You Should Quit Reddit

Jacob Desforges

www.jacobdesforges.com

Independently published.

ISBN-13: 978-1-0881-4562-3

Disclaimer: This work is compiled from the author's own views and opinions derived from personal experience as a user of the website www.reddit.com, combined with research from third-party sources. The author is not and has never been associated with Reddit, Incorporated (or its parent company Advance Publications) in any capacity other than as a user of their site. Any conclusions drawn by the author regarding the opinions, beliefs, motivations, or actions of Reddit, Incorporated or its affiliates (past or present) should be considered to be conjecture, other than text which is explicitly attributed to said entity with a direct quote.

Table of Contents

Introduction

Ironically, those most in need of this book may be the most difficult to convince to pick it up and read it (or any book for that matter). Their attention spans have atrophied. Their brain's reward circuitry has been hijacked by an addictive social media platform. Four sentences in, they may already be subconsciously itching to put down this book and navigate back to Reddit.

I know them so well because I was one of them. A Redditor. An addict. As a user of Reddit for over a decade, I know all too well how the site can suck away your free time and mental energy. Some days I spent thirty minutes on the site; some days I spent four or five hours. This book will focus specifically on Reddit as that is the platform which I am most familiar with, although many of the conclusions are applicable to other social media platforms and internet communities.

When most people think of addiction, they think of a drug user or an alcoholic. Comparatively, the field of research into internet and social media addiction is in its relative infancy. These fall under the broader category of behavioral addiction or process addiction, which psychologists would define as a form of addiction that involves a compulsion to engage in a rewarding non-substance-related behavior despite any negative consequences to the person's physical, mental, social, or financial well-being.

Note that there is no minimum amount of time that one would have to spend on internet surfing activities like Reddit for it to qualify as a behavioral addiction. The two qualifiers are that the behavior is physiologically rewarding (which as we will examine in this book, Reddit certainly is) and that one continues to engage in the behavior despite experiencing negative consequences as a result of their use. The severity of those consequences is what determines the stigma with which the afflicted individual is viewed by society and themselves. A gambler losing his home and life savings, thus putting his family out on the street, would certainly be viewed in a more negative light than someone who simply burns all of their free time on surfing the internet after work.

However, this relative lack of outward evident harm is what enables internet use addiction to be so insidious. We may feel guilty for wasting our evenings on the internet rather than spending our time on activities which are more productive, enjoyable, and valuable to our personal growth. But due to the fact that in the vast majority of cases of internet addiction one is simply stunting their maximum potential and not actively harming their existing lifestyle (e.g. career, finances, and relationships) they are unlikely to experience a rock-bottom moment which may compel them to true introspection.

I was the poster child for this moderate level of internet addiction in that my usage of Reddit had clearly not ruined my life. I discovered and joined Reddit shortly before college, and in the approximately eleven years that followed my best guess of my Reddit usage is around three hours per day on average. During this same period I started and completed an engineering degree, landed and held down a career with a respectable salary, and maintained a long-term relationship.

Clearly I am doing just fine when measured by these common metrics that our society uses to measure outward life success at a glance. And to be honest, I used this as an excuse to justify to myself why it didn't matter that I wasted so much of my time surfing Reddit — and at times, why I *deserved* to do so. This seems to be a common thread of denialism among people who have some level of digital addiction. In a YouTube video posted by video game streamer "sunpi" where she gives a counter-argument to *Game Quitters* founder and former gaming addict Cam Adair's reasoning for why people should quit video games, the comment section is full of people offering a similar type of flawed logic which I formerly subscribed to. Users justify their daily gaming habit with reasons such as being able to simultaneously complete college, holding down a career that they claim is successful, taking time to work out, or (my personal favorite response) because they are a homeowner and an investor. In my opinion this comment section offered a great window into a sample of digital addicts in denial, as there's likely no overlap between the group of people who have a balanced relationship with gaming and those who think about it so much that they spend *additional* time watching other people play and talk about video games.

As I moved into my mid-20s, I began to feel that my internet usage was impinging on my ability to get more out of life. I envied people who had the drive to dedicate a large chunk of their free time to a hobby or craft that resulted in a sense of satisfaction and tangible accomplishment. I always had ideas for things that I would like to pursue, but they almost always lost out to the lower activation energy activity of opening Reddit. I was no longer satisfied with hedonistic contentment but instead sought fulfillment. It wasn't that my internet use was causing me to end up in the left tail of the socioeconomic distribution (i.e. a statistical loser) but rather that it was dampening my potential to accomplish more and live a more meaningful and present life, things which I knew that I was capable of with some dedicated effort.

A few of the recent years of my life were marked by a commitment to try and live more intentionally by spending less time surfing the web and instead redirecting those hours into the activities I had always thought about doing. I started a blog about financial independence to share knowledge and chronicle my progress. I bought a guitar and started practicing regularly. I began reading books for pleasure again, something I hadn't done since high school. I tried my hand at homebrewing beer. It was amazing to me how much time I had left in the day after completely cutting Reddit and similar "boredom surfing" out of my life.

If it were that simple to instantly quit wasting time on the internet, I would not be writing this book. For over two years, I would yo-yo between the same cycle:

1. Delete my Reddit account and stop going on the site completely, then re-commit myself to using my time more intentionally and focusing the vast majority of my free time towards self-development and more rewarding, productive hobbies.

2. A few days to two weeks later, tentatively venture back onto Reddit to check up on my favorite communities on the site (usually justifying to myself that there's no harm in killing twenty to thirty minutes just once).

3. Eventually create a new Reddit account so I can vote, comment, and customize my home feed. Gradually get sucked back into spending more time on the site until I'm back to sinking two-plus hours per day into it.

4. A couple of months later, realize that my use of Reddit has once again consumed the lion's share of my free time and that my hobbies have languished. Proceed back to step one.

It took two iterations of this cycle for me to realize it for what it truly was — the cycle of addiction. Experiencing that relapse step in real-time was the key insight. The vast majority of social media users have never attempted to quit their services of choice completely. If they do have cognitive dissonance about their level of social media usage, "I can quit whenever I want" is likely a common refrain, which is the stereotypical mantra of an addict. Specifically with regard to Reddit, compounding this issue is that there is debate among users about whether Reddit even qualifies as social media at all! Looking back at archived posts of Redditors debating this topic, post-2018 (when Reddit rolled out a new site design that was uncannily similar to Facebook's user interface), seems to be a tipping point towards most users finally conceding that the site is indeed a social media platform.

At some point after yet another cycle of relapse and wasting the majority of a weekend on Reddit, I grew frustrated beyond belief. Why was nobody talking about how addictive this site is? What was wrong with *me* specifically that I could not stop impulsively using Reddit when I often found little of value on the site? Was I so weak-willed that I was the only loser that couldn't just simply choose to walk away from a website and stick to it?

As I discovered, it turns out there was a group of people talking about it over on the /r/NoSurf subreddit. NoSurf describes itself as "a community of people who are focused on becoming more productive and wasting less time mindlessly surfing the internet." There I found some kindred spirits facing the same struggles, sharing tips as they attempted to break the cycle of behavioral addiction that they had developed with internet use. While I learned quite a bit from the /r/NoSurf community, it was not the source of the answers that I sought. Apparently many people there were in the same boat, as users frequently submitted posts confessing to falling into the same cycle of deleting and recreating accounts on Reddit and other platforms, as well as reporting a general difficulty figuring out how to permanently reform their technology habits.

My frustrations culminated in a revelation that anyone who had successfully quit Reddit would not be coming back to the site to share with everyone else how they did it. By definition, there would be an inverse relationship between how successful one was at cutting down their web browsing and that person's likelihood of hanging out on internet forums to chat with strangers. I vowed that if I ever came to the answer myself, I would create a resource to share with others how to do the same. This book is that product, and as an added benefit is completely offline.

After a lot of thinking, I finally realized that simply attempting to quit Reddit abruptly was not going to be effective if I did not diagnose and overpower the subconscious compulsion to return to the site. My cognitive dissonance was a clash between the addictive hooks of modern social media platforms versus the recognition that my time spent on Reddit was of *negative* value because not only was I frequently annoyed with Reddit and its users while browsing the site, but it was also actively impeding my pursuit of other goals. To tip the scales I would need to begin by consciously examining each and every one of my own actions and motivations rather than letting my subconscious run on autopilot. This involved looking at when and why I felt compelled to use Reddit, and what the expected versus actual outcome of using the site was. The resulting product was a sort of "Theory of Reddit" explaining why users like me were drawn to the site and what (if any) value proposition it offered to users.

Part I of this book will guide you through that reframing process. We will begin by examining the structure of Reddit as a pseudonymous social media platform and how this introduces a unique flavor of addictiveness to the site. We will then take a detailed look at the digital culture that has sprung up on Reddit, posit some reasoning for why Redditors behave in the way that they do, and answer the question of whether these are people that we should be spending time with. Next, we will describe the different types of content that one is likely to find when browsing Reddit, and dispel some common misconceptions that hold corners of the site as sources of knowledge and entertainment. We'll learn how Reddit has evolved over time, explaining why the site seems to have tended towards even lower value content and interactions in recent years. I will also peel back the curtain on some of the more nefarious activities such as inauthentic manipulation of content and even flagrant abuses of power by site moderators and administrators, and what implications these hold for users and the future of Reddit.

Finally, I will wrap up Part I by sharing the abundance of positive changes that I have noted in my own life since quitting Reddit and all other social media platforms, for the purpose of giving my readers an idea of what they serve to gain by doing the same. While most other large social media platforms have in recent years had a plethora of attention directed at the negative impacts that they have caused on their users and society, Reddit has — until now — been able to mostly fly under the radar of public opinion despite engaging in some of the same practices that have created widespread outcry directed at platforms like Facebook, Twitter, Instagram, TikTok, and others. The goal of Part I is to give you a lens through which to lay bare all the flaws of Reddit and similar time-wasting sites, such that you have mental ammunition with which to coherently articulate why you should break away from them. Some of what I write will come off as highly critical, but these are the conclusions that I have arrived at after being a Redditor for over a decade.

Part II of this book will focus on the *how*. It will give you the tools and techniques to quit visiting time-wasting websites like Reddit for good, so you can effectively reclaim your time to use in a more intentional manner. I will describe how I shattered the cycle of addiction and relapse that caused me to repeatedly get sucked back into using these sites before I finally learned how to walk away. Ultimately, I had to redefine my relationship with the internet, and to some extent with technology as a whole.

This book was written from the perspective of — and for maximum benefit to — someone who has struggled to quit or reduce the amount of time that they spend on Reddit and other time-wasting web scrolling activities. It may also be highly beneficial to regular or occasional users of Reddit who are open to questioning the value of the site, and I daresay it could even be interesting to those who are only casually acquainted with Reddit but desire to spend less time online in general. Many of us have spent years on these platforms and received little of substance in return to show for it; in fact, they have cost us the opportunity to live more fulfilling, present, and interesting lives. This is hardly a surprising outcome since (as we will learn) the average adult is investing the temporal equivalent of a part-time job into scrolling and consuming media on their various devices. It's time to decide whether you want more out of life than that.

If this book helps just a handful of people who are in a similar situation as I was, then it will have been worth writing.

Part I:

A Theory of Reddit

Chapter 1
Why You Keep Scrolling

Do you often find that you've opened a browser tab or picked up your phone and navigated to Reddit almost subconsciously? In my years of Reddit use, I'd often just "find" myself on Reddit when I was procrastinating a task, or when I was bored. I would end up scrolling for five, ten, fifteen minutes in a zombified state before I came back to reality, closed the tab, and got back to what I should have been doing. Then as soon as I hit a mental interruption in my work flow, there I went: right back to Reddit. This was a common theme across many stages in my life: back in college staring at homework problems I should be starting; when I was at work in former jobs and didn't have any immediate deadlines; at home procrastinating a chore or deflecting using my free time for productive or enriching purposes. In all cases, straight to Reddit.

What is it about Reddit and other sites serving content on an infinite scroll that sucks us in, oftentimes to the point where we find ourselves incessantly opening the site a dozen or more times per day? Laziness and the desire to procrastinate certainly play a role. But these sites are also exploiting our behavioral psychology, taking advantage of mechanisms that are hard-coded into our brains by millions of years of evolution and which began being studied in earnest by behaviorists around the turn of the twentieth century. Operant conditioning is a type of associative learning process through which the strength of a behavior is modified by reinforcement or punishment, originated by Edward Thorndike as a distinct differentiation from Ivan Pavlov's model of classical conditioning (which dealt with involuntary behaviors). You may have also heard of B.F. Skinner, who placed rats in boxes with levers and studied the effects of rewarding or punishing them for pressing the lever. Skinner found that rewarding the rats with food for pressing the lever strengthened their desire to do so, and punishing them with an electric shock weakened or eliminated their desire to press the lever.

Skinner did an extensive analysis of the results from delivering reinforcements in various arrangements over time, publishing the results in his book *Schedules of Reinforcement* in 1957. For our purposes of examining parallels to Reddit, the most relevant of Skinner's schedules of reinforcement is the variable ratio schedule. Under this model, the rat would be rewarded with food after pressing the lever a random amount of times, for example ten times, then thirty times, then five times. The reward would be delivered after an unpredictable number of actions. When the food was removed, the rats that were conditioned under the variable reinforcement group were found to engage in the lever-pressing behavior long after the rats that were continuously reinforced by getting a reward for every lever press. Because the variable ratio rats were conditioned to engage in a behavior with an uncertain amount of actions prior to their next reward — but also were conditioned to learn they were *eventually* guaranteed to get a reward with persistent effort — their learned behaviors ended up being more resilient.

Now consider your time spent browsing Reddit. You don't

enjoy every post. Most are just mediocre and you quickly move past them. But you subconsciously have learned that if you keep scrolling, you will eventually find a funny meme, an insightful post, or a seemingly knowledgeable comment. You don't know when it's coming, but experience has taught you that if you keep scrolling, you will eventually find something enjoyable. You may have to scroll past five uninteresting or mediocre posts before finding one that really appeals to you, and then perhaps you need to scroll past three, or even ten more posts before replicating that feeling again. But you subconsciously recognize that if you keep scrolling, you will eventually be rewarded with entertainment or information that matches your expectations and leads to an enjoyable experience. Redditors are analogous to the rats in Skinner's operant conditioning chambers, participating in a variable ratio reinforcement experiment.

There's a lot of flak rightfully being directed at social media platforms that use algorithms designed to increase our engagement by manipulating our emotions or using behavioral psychology tricks. Their ultimate goal of course is to keep one's eyeballs on their site as long as possible and encourage users to come back more frequently such that they see more advertisements and thus generate more revenue. What these companies stumbled onto was likely unintentional. The state of social media platforms today is the natural product of profit-seeking organizations happening to make various design decisions that appealed to their users on a subconscious level and then hyper-optimizing for the most effective, engaging system — all while competing in a marketplace where other social media companies (their competitors) are doing exactly the same thing out of self-interest. The logical expected outcome of intentionally attempting to design a system for maximum addictive potential based on human psychology versus A/B testing various innocuous design choices then selecting the one that is most engaging to users is similar, as the users will spend more time on the version of the site that is more enticing and thus cause development to progress towards increasingly addictive iterations.

I think it's important to note that there isn't *necessarily* anything malicious (at least that which can be attributed to a single person or group) about the fact that Reddit acts as a digital Skinner Box, feeding us content in the most behaviorally addicting manner. It's simply a logical consequence of a single platform that offers such a broad range of content. Even after curating the site towards our interests by subscribing to different subreddit communities, how well individual submissions fit our *idea* of the content that we expect to see in that community, as well as the wide disparity in the quality of submissions will still create that variable ratio reinforcement schedule.

Several users of the /r/NoSurf community on Reddit admit to ingesting the wealth of information offered on the site in an obsessive manner. They derive temporary feelings of productivity by finding nuggets of knowledge and learning things while scrolling the internet. Because they convinced themselves that they weren't using Reddit solely for entertainment purposes, these users deluded themselves for years into believing that their time spent on the site was less wasteful than it truly was. Many describe arriving at a sudden, shattering revelation upon realizing that despite continuously reading and cataloging, they never actually *do* anything with the information that they've acquired. Some sources refer to this as compulsive information seeking; others call it information addiction.

Upon reflecting on my own usage of Reddit over the prior decade or so, I also saw evidence of this behavior. For a couple of years I was subscribed to the /r/LearnProgramming subreddit. I had an interest in learning at least some basic computer programming, so I joined the community and its posts became part of my Reddit feed. I would occasionally read the /r/LearnProgramming posts and comments when they came across my feed, yet I had never taken any action to actually implement that knowledge and start somewhere with programming. Taking a closer look at several of the subreddits that I had subscribed to, I noticed that they fit the same pattern. It turned out that I was a compulsive information seeker as well.

Those users on /r/NoSurf acknowledging their own problems may be some of the most introspective, self-honest users of Reddit, and their stories likely represent just the tip of the iceberg. How many other Redditors are experiencing varying degrees of information addiction? As much as some users like to believe that Reddit remains a niche little club on the web, it has certainly gone mainstream — the site consistently ranks in the top twenty websites visited worldwide and the top ten in the United States, and in 2020 Chief Operating Officer Jen Wong disclosed to *The Wall Street Journal* that Reddit had fifty-two million daily active users.[1] Certainly some number of those daily users are spending an unhealthy amount of time on the site, compelled by a subconscious psychological motive to return day after day.

The success and allure of Reddit are due in large part to its uniqueness; nowhere else on the internet can you so easily assemble a personally-curated feed of thriving communities focusing on several disparate interests. Upon discovering that some subreddit dedicated to a highly obscure topic exists, Redditors will commonly quip, "there's a subreddit for everything!" Users can subscribe to communities focused on news and current events; hobbies such as fitness, travel, and video games; lifestyle communities focused on a singular topic like minimalism or frugality; advice for improving motivation and productivity; discussion of their career field; following their favorite media franchises; countless numbers of subreddits dedicated to entertainment where jokes, memes, and videos from around the internet are shared, and so much more — all aggregated and mixed together into a singular and sometimes hectic feed. But it's *your* feed, consisting likely of dozens of communities that collectively define you as an individual. Users who find the concept of Reddit appealing tend to make the site their primary hangout online, often receiving a majority of their information from it.

If one is subscribed to a large number of communities on Reddit, they can open the site several hours apart and find a completely different feed of posts waiting for them. This continuous promise of novelty mingled with the fear of missing out had me navigating to Reddit multiple times per day; some days I opened the site over a dozen times. Once a user is on the site, they will then perform their learned behavior to continue scrolling. The content feed rewarding users akin to a variable ratio reinforcement schedule provides a strong psychological imperative to persist in scrolling, subconsciously encouraging users to stay on Reddit.

Armed with the knowledge of how Reddit and similar platforms exploit our behavioral psychology to keep us scrolling, we can more intentionally examine our interactions with these sites. When you find a post humorous, is it *actually* funny, or only by relative comparison to the plethora of low-effort, stale humor that is so prevalent on the site? When you find a comment informative, how do you know if it is truly accurate? Are you actually going to apply that knowledge to something in your life? When a post or comment elicits an emotional reaction from you, how often is it positive versus negative, and how does that impact your attitude and mood for the remainder of your day?

Perhaps most importantly, can you even remember the last

time you found something truly valuable or impactful to your life on Reddit? If so, consider the amount of time that you had to spend scrolling through low-value content to find these few items. It's probably not unlike finding a needle in a haystack — except the hay in this example is your finite time on the planet being thrown to the wind.

Chapter 2
Karma Crack

While most social media platforms use "likes" to serve as the main barometer of success for users' posts, Reddit uses a system known as karma. In their own help documentation, Reddit describes karma as "a reflection of how much your contributions mean to the community."[2] Likes and karma share the same concept. Similar to all other social platforms, Reddit users can vote on posts and comments; each user can vote on items only once, and thus all users have equivalent power. However, karma is different from the likes on other social media platforms in distinct ways which amplify these platforms' inherent flaws and ensures that Reddit is at least as addictive as the rest of them.

One way in which Reddit's karma system is different is that a user's total score is displayed on their profile. This is broken down into "post karma" and "comment karma" to respectively differentiate users' scores for top-level content they have submitted to the site's feed, versus their scores for interacting in the comment section of those submissions. Facebook, Twitter, and Instagram do not display a user's total like count anywhere on the site, so this makes Reddit's implementation fairly unique. Some Redditors pride themselves on having millions of karma as a bellwether for the amount of value they have contributed to the site over the years. In a thread asking other users why they are addicted to gathering karma, one person responds, "Karma on Reddit tells me that what I have to say on my opinions and beliefs is valid, and that other people actually *enjoyed* reading my perspective."

Speaking from my own experience, when I first joined Reddit back in 2010 or so I was seventeen years old. At that time I cared quite a bit about my karma total, and I put effort into commenting and posting things that I thought would increase my score. I went so far as to delete submissions that did poorly from my account history to protect my karma score from further damage as well as to give the impression that I only posted things that were positively received — therefore implying that all the opinions and beliefs that I held were "correct," even in my personal life beyond Reddit. As I grew older and gained more experience on Reddit, I stopped caring about my total account karma score since I realized it was a poor proxy for measuring how much total value a user had contributed. Someone who posted funny jokes in the site's largest communities, for example, would inevitably end up with more points than someone writing detailed informational posts in smaller knowledge-oriented subreddits, simply due to the magnitude of difference in the number of users that would see and vote on each contribution.

However, even the above realization did not completely break me free from caring about karma and only shifted my perspective. I instead cared about how my individual submissions and comments scored *relative* to the communities that they were posted in. For example, in a smaller subreddit, getting a submission to the number one slot as rated by "hot" posts may require only a hundred positive votes. In Reddit's largest communities, this feat would require tens of thousands or hundreds of thousands of users to "upvote" (i.e. like) your submission.

After submitting posts or comments, I would frequently return to Reddit to check my account history and see how the karma scores of my submissions developed over the next several hours. I would also excitedly look for that little orange envelope notification which indicated that another user had replied to my content. Even though I honestly could claim to not care about the total karma score of my account, for many years I still cared that my individual posts garnered positive reception and engagement as a barometer of social validation of my opinions and beliefs. This is not a unique phenomenon to Reddit and is observed as a motivator of participation across users of all social media platforms.

Research in the cognitive neuroscience field confirms underlying mechanisms in the brain that encourage the type of behavior that I engaged in. Receiving likes on one's social media content is associated with greater activation of the brain's reward circuitry, and activation in a region known as the "social brain" was also observed.[3] The social brain is a collection of structures that support complex social interactions and are involved in understanding other people. These functions include things such as social perception, signaling, and social drive (e.g. how to increase one's own status in the social hierarchy).[4]

In comparison to the timeline of human evolution, the existence of social media platforms is an inconceivably tiny blip. What may have started off as an innocuous invention ended up tapping into deep-rooted pathways within our brains that our evolution self-selected for. Our ancestors who organized into complex societies would have had higher survival rates than lone individuals or small groups, and it's conceivable that those who were able to accurately ascertain their relative position in society and felt driven to increase their standing were more likely to reproduce. We are thus compelled to want to connect with each other, and social media offers that ability on perhaps a grander scale — both in the number of potential connections and the speed of interactions — than anything before in human history.

The second and most apparent way in which Reddit's karma system is distinct from other social media platforms is that users can "downvote" posts and comments. Most other social media platforms do not have a button for negative feedback. For example, there is no dislike button on Facebook, Twitter, or Instagram. YouTube was previously the largest website that had a "dislike" option in the form of a thumbs down button. However in late 2021, YouTube hid the statistics that previously indicated both the number and percentage of users who had disliked a particular video from public view, leaving them accessible only to the video's publisher. Reddit now stands alone among the top-ranking websites with social interaction features as the only one to offer a negative feedback button.

Reddit's help documentation states that users should use the downvote feature on posts and comments if they "think it does not contribute to the subreddit it is posted in or is off-topic in a particular community."[5] However, users of the site seem to nearly unanimously agree that in practice, the downvote button is more frequently used to indicate *disagreement* with a post or comment rather than whether it detracts from the discussion.

Top-level posts cannot go below zero karma, but comments have no negative lower bound. Just as a user's positive (upvoted) contributions count towards their total account karma score, their negative (downvoted) contributions will subtract from it. Users with net-negative scoring comments will see karma deducted from the total shown on their profile.

When a comment hits a score of negative five, it is automatically collapsed and hidden. Other users must specifically choose to click and expand each comment at or below this threshold if they wish to view it. Additionally, if a user has a low or negative karma score in a specific subreddit community, that user will be restricted to commenting only once per every ten minutes. These features can be a positive when dealing with spambots or vitriolic and abusive trolls who are better off out of sight and out of mind. In other cases, they can serve to amplify the flaws of Reddit as a social platform.

Because users tend to downvote information that they disagree with, the downvoting system is prone to being weaponized to suppress comments which are presented respectfully, but that the majority of users in that community disagree with. Oftentimes, any opinion that differs from the majority will be downvoted; for example, Reddit famously has a strong left-leaning political bias, and even the most tactful countering arguments from someone of a differing opinion are prone to being annihilated with downvotes. But beyond opinions, at times factually correct information is downvoted as well. This can be as simple as an expert in a hobby subreddit attempting to explain some nuanced exception where the community's common knowledge is incorrect, to more insidious situations where verifiable facts are downvoted by users because they present an inconvenient truth that invalidates the core beliefs of a community and triggers cognitive dissonance.

The way the downvoting system on Reddit functions and the manner in which many users weaponize it are the main drivers for the widespread criticism that many communities on Reddit are echo chambers. An echo chamber refers to situations in which beliefs are amplified or reinforced by communication and repetition inside a closed system and insulated from rebuttal. Existing beliefs are repeated by users seeking social validation. Those who dissent are partially silenced by having their content downvoted until it is hidden (and then receive still further negative votes by additional users who use the button to signal their disapproval). Users who care about receiving positive karma scores on their content as a measure of social validation will be pressured to change their beliefs to conform with the community. They would avoid posting content that a community may find disagreeable or controversial to avoid garnering downvotes, and instead stick to posting "safe" comments which reflect the existing beliefs of the community. Users who refuse to conform will eventually have their ability to participate restricted once their karma score in a particular subreddit sinks low enough to trigger the one comment per ten minutes limitation.

The term "echo chamber" in reference to Reddit is most frequently used by critics of the site's strong left-leaning political bias. However, my assertion is that echo chambers on Reddit do not just form around highly opinionated and contentious topics like politics. The karma system of the site enables communities centered around even the most innocuous of subjects to become echo chambers. In my past experience on Reddit I have found strong elements of echo chambers in subreddits related to personal finance, real estate, and even slow cookers! For example, the /r/RealEstate community is primarily populated with people who work in that industry such as real estate agents and mortgage brokers, as well as individual homeowners who want to keep up with the market. All of these users have a vested interest in home prices appreciating, so they tend to upvote information that supports this conclusion while downvoting and castigating anybody who posts data or hypotheses indicating that home prices might decline.

Some users claim to have fully divorced themselves from caring about their karma score or the social validation that it represents, and just post whatever is on their mind without regard to how it will be perceived by others. For the latter few years of my tenure on Reddit, I had reached what I thought was this admirable state of self-confidence and nonchalance. I posted my honest thoughts about topics and wasn't bothered by occasionally eating downvotes after attempting to correct misinformation, especially in technically-oriented subreddits where the truth should be more objective.

I viewed myself as above the petty karma system of Reddit and the poor interaction quality that it self-selects for. Of course, this was only a half-formed train of thought, produced while I was only part of the way down the path to realizing what a waste of my time participating on Reddit in any capacity was. In the end, users who claim not to care about karma but continue to post on the site are still subjecting themselves to an environment where the karma system is shaping how other users interact with them, and allowing such "community policing" to determine if people ultimately see what one posts. As much as one might like to believe that they are personally indifferent to karma, they cannot truly escape its effects as long as they continue to participate on Reddit.

The karma system is a core feature of Reddit and is nearly inseparable from the site's identity. It serves to increase the addictive nature of the site which has likely contributed to Reddit's success and popularity, and it has also had a powerful influence on developing the unique culture of Redditors. Overall, the impacts of this system work out to be generally beneficial to Reddit and their business strategy, but likely negative for the site's users. Consciously recognizing the ways in which this system manipulates human behavior should cause you to question whether this is an environment worth participating in at all.

Chapter 3
The Average Redditor

Anyone who has used Reddit for even a short period of time has likely seen multiple people make a reference to the "average Redditor." Every user likely has a slightly different definition of the average Redditor, however the general concept is that they constitute a group of users who have distinct identifying characteristics and mannerisms that are unique to Reddit's culture compared to other websites, and whom one is likely to encounter when participating on the site. When this phrase is brought up it is nearly always in a derogatory manner, and the average Redditor is commonly associated with having a collection of traits and engaging in behaviors which the referencing user finds irritating, off-putting, or indicative of stupidity. Users almost universally agree that they imagine the average Redditor physically as a young American white male, as this is the site's most common demographic. Behavior-wise, average Redditors are frequently accused of having a superiority complex, possessing stunted social skills, and eagerly engaging in arguments (especially over semantics) with other users.

Throughout Reddit's history there have been multiple communities created with the sole purpose of making fun of the culture of Reddit and its users; some have grown to have six-figure subscriber counts like /r/RedditMoment, while several others such as /r/AverageRedditor were banned from Reddit by the site's administrators with the reasoning that they were violating rules against harassment. Across Reddit, critical comments denigrating the average Redditor are often highly upvoted. On the surface it may seem paradoxical that comments insulting the average user of the site quite often see such highly positive reception as measured by upvotes, however a couple of different effects may explain this.

The first effect is likely due to a social psychology term known as illusory superiority, which is a cognitive bias wherein a person overestimates their own qualities and abilities in relation to the same qualities and abilities of other people. Surveys are frequently used to demonstrate this bias, such as one survey of Master of Business Administration (MBA) students at Stanford University, which found that eighty-seven percent of students rated their own academic performance as being above the median. Since by definition the median is the fiftieth percentile of a data set, it would be impossible for more than half of the students to be in this range. Similar surveys have been performed on car drivers and found that the vast majority rated themselves as safer than average.

Likewise, illusory superiority also causes people to underestimate their negative qualities in relation to others, which is highly relevant here because many of the traits and behaviors attributed to the average Redditor are negative. For example, a user who engages in arguments with others on the internet more frequently than average would tend to underplay their tendency to do so. Due to illusory superiority, it is plausible that a significant amount of the derision for average Redditors comes from users who perfectly fit that mold themselves!

The second effect, which I believe is a larger factor than the former, may be explained by people mistakenly assuming that the interactions of other users with the site follow a uniform distribution. For example, users may assume that when they leave a comment on Reddit, that every other user of the site is roughly equally likely to reply to their comment. Many users likely believe that their aggregate experience over months or years of interactions with other users — primarily by viewing their posts and reading their comments — can be distilled down to give them an accurate picture of the average Redditor.

However, this premise is flawed because the number of interactions per user does not follow a uniform distribution, it follows a power law distribution. The Pareto Principle is a useful aphorism for explaining the basic concepts of power law distributions. The Pareto Principle states that for any given event, eighty percent of outcomes (or outputs) are due to twenty percent of all causes (or inputs). Applied to Reddit, this would mean that eighty percent of all comments you read on the site come from just twenty percent of Redditors.

Of course, the Pareto Principle is just a rough observation which many natural and man-made systems have been observed to generally adhere to. For example, the richest twenty percent of the world's people make roughly eighty percent of the income, and manufacturers have noted that the most successful twenty percent of their products constitute eighty percent of their revenue. We cannot conclusively use it to assert that twenty percent of commenters leave eighty percent of the comments on Reddit; that latter number may be sixty percent, ninety percent, or something else. In the absence of Reddit releasing detailed user data (which they likely will never do, as that data is at the core of their business model), the Pareto Principle provides a rough guideline.

Further evidence that Reddit's number of interactions per user generally follows a power law distribution can be gleaned from time-on-site data. Website traffic analytics site *Similarweb* reports that the average duration of a visit to Reddit was ten minutes[6], and although data on the average number of visits per day was not provided this number *must* be greater than one — since anybody making zero visits would not be counted in the data — which would serve as a multiplier when determining the average total time per user spent on the site each day. Reddit's own advertising information page used to provide some incredibly basic data about their audience from 2020. From there, we learn that users of the official Reddit smartphone app spent on average thirty-four minutes daily in the app.[7]

On that same page, Reddit also claimed to have a device breakdown of seventy-three percent mobile users and twenty-seven percent Personal Computer users. With nearly a three-to-one ratio, it may be reasonable to assume that for Reddit users who access the site via the smartphone app, this represents most of their time on the site. However, the argument can also be made that sampling those who are willing to download the Reddit app is biasing towards people who care more about the site and thus were already spending an above-average amount of time on it. Additionally, Reddit has a motivation to cherry-pick the highest time-on-site metric they can find in order to look as appealing as possible to advertisers.

Given all of the above factors, I find it reasonable and conservative to assume that the average Reddit user spends about a half hour daily on the site. Consider that context against a user like myself; in the over a decade I spent on Reddit, I estimate that my average daily usage was in the realm of three hours. I spent around **six times** longer on Reddit each day than the average user!

Consequentially, you would be about six times more likely to see a post or to read a comment written by me than one created by the average Redditor. I would be about six times more likely to view *your* post or comment and vote on it or reply to it than the average Redditor would. This of course assumes things like equivalent typing speed and similar motivation to comment or post on the site versus just "lurking," which are gross simplifications that we will rectify later in this book. For now, this is sufficient for the purposes of proving the general existence of a power law distribution in the number of interactions attributable to each Reddit user.

You can imagine then the sheer volume of posts and comments that can be output by outlier users who spend five or more hours per day on Reddit. They are each getting the same amount of visibility as ten or more average users! An appropriate term to refer to these outliers would be "power Redditors." The thoughts, opinions, and mannerisms of these power Redditors in many cases may not represent those of the average Redditor. In fact, power Redditors may be nearly completely responsible for the poor reputation of the average Redditor; I don't think it's controversial to assume that there is a positive correlation between how much time a person spends online and their likelihood of being maladjusted.

Therefore, the term "average Redditor" is a colloquialism, and when people use this term (whether they know it or not), they are generalizing a stereotype of most Redditors from the archetypical interactions that they feel they are most likely to experience on the site. Once one understands that, it becomes clear that the negative behaviors and traits often attributed to the average user of Reddit may actually be mostly attributable to a small percentage of users who spend an outsized amount of time on the site. The power Redditors are giving a bad name to the average Redditor through the fallacy of faulty generalization.

The users that the community actually collectively detests are the power Redditors, some of whom spend enough time on the site daily to rival a full-time job (plus overtime on the weekends). We already know quite a bit about this subset of users, as I have proven that the behaviors previously attributed to the colloquial average Redditor truly just belong to the power Redditors. They're the type of people who are *proud* to use Reddit, consider being a Redditor part of their personal identity, and fully immerse themselves in the site's culture. They're the ones spending hours per day arguing online (with that characteristic insufferable smarmy attitude that one can't quite find anywhere but Reddit) to compensate for deep-rooted insecurities related to their own intelligence. Likewise, they are also the reason why Redditors are characterized as misanthropic — thanks to the power law distribution, a small number of terminally online, *actual* misanthropes can drown out the opinions of the much larger crowd of "normal" people each spending a fraction of the amount of time on Reddit per day.

Power Redditors are truly the worst-behaved users that the site has to offer. Reddit is a mainstream website now, but I recall that for the first decade or so of its existence, casual browsers of the site would be embarrassed to publicly admit that they used Reddit out of fear of being associated with its user base. Whether you're a power Redditor yourself who is seeking rehabilitation, a casual user of the site who is simply tired of its culture, or something in between like I was, chances are that you're reading this book because you've experienced (or suspect) that Reddit may be having a negative impact on your life. Debunking the colloquialism of the average Redditor and properly assigning these behaviors to the power Redditors does not change the fact that you will continue to encounter them with the same frequency if you keep using Reddit.

If you believe that we become more like the people whom we spend our time with, this realization may be all that is needed to spur you into cutting the cord with Reddit. If you instead believe that you can continue using Reddit without having the traits of its users rub off on you, why would you *want* to hang out with such people and even offer them a chance to bring their negativity into your life? These conclusions are not just relevant to Reddit and can be extrapolated to any online social space where users can interact with each other, and should serve as a prompt to begin more closely scrutinizing the value proposition of all of your online activities. As far as Reddit goes, though, to understand why these users behave in the way that they do and how being a "Redditor" evolved as a unique digital subculture necessitates starting from the site's founding back in 2005.

Chapter 4
An Uncultured Culture

Digital social groups have the ability to form their own unique cultures, just as we have historical evidence that physical social groups have done so for millennia. Culture in its broadest sense is a collection of cultivated behaviors; that is, the totality of a person's learned, accumulated experience that is socially transmitted. To understand the roots of Reddit's culture, we need to go back to the earliest days of the site. By taking a look at the initial people that founded the site and then those who "settled" virtually on Reddit — especially what behaviors they brought with them to the site — we will identify some of the cultural norms of Reddit that have been passed down to today as new users have assimilated to the site over the years.

Reddit.com was founded and launched in June 2005 by Alexis Ohanian and Steve Huffman while they were roommates together at the University of Virginia. The site was initially conceived as a bulletin board for news. The Wayback Machine internet archive project has the earliest preserved page of Reddit from July 25, 2005. Looking at this, I noted the simplicity of the initial iteration of Reddit compared to today:

- There were no subreddit communities. Every post was submitted to the main Reddit page, which was identical for all users.
- Users could only submit URLs linking to other websites, and there were no such things as posts containing text, image, or video content.
- The vast majority of links were to news articles reporting current (at the time) world events, as well as websites and blogs sharing technology news.
- Users had two reaction buttons to posts: "interesting" and "not interesting," which determined the sorting of links by net user reactions. This is a clear precursor to the karma system of today which has upvotes and downvotes.
- There were no comments. The only manner in which users could interact with each other was through voting on links.

Simpler times indeed! Reddit back then was arguably not a social media site, perhaps only in the vaguest stretch of the word. This may partially explain some early users' opposition (still persisting today, to a lesser degree) towards accepting that Reddit is now a social media platform, even as the site continued to evolve more strongly in that direction over the years.

Internet archive content from the beginning days of Reddit paints a picture of a small but active community. Of the top twenty-five links on Reddit from the July 25, 2005 snapshot, over half were submitted by one single account, however eight other users round out the submitters of the top twenty-five links. As time moves forward, we see in an August 14, 2005 snapshot that thirteen different usernames are responsible for submitting the top twenty-five links.

Who were these Redditors in the first few months of the

site getting off the ground? Well, actually, it was mostly just two dudes. The founders of Reddit created a bunch of fake accounts to submit most of these links in order to give the appearance of a thriving community. This isn't a conspiracy theory; it was confirmed by one of the Reddit co-founders, Steve Huffman. In a 2012 course that he taught about web development on *Udacity*, Huffman admits to this and explains how the process worked in the lesson "Growing Reddit":

> In the beginning, Alexis and I submitted all the content. If you go to our Reddit submission page now, it basically boils down to two fields. And in the early days it was just two fields. You basically had a field called 'URL' which is the URL of the site you were submitting, and 'Title,' which was the title of that site, and that would be the link you submitted to Reddit. If Alexis and I went to the page we had a third field called 'User,' and we could type in a name here, and when we hit submit, we would automatically register this user if that name didn't exist and submit the content as that user. So you'd go to Reddit in the early days, the first couple of months, and there would be tons of content. I shouldn't say 'fake content,' but it was fake users. It was really all just Alexis and I.[8]

Huffman goes on to explain how this went on for a few months before inertia took over and they didn't have to submit any content because actual users had begun doing so organically, and how their initial manipulation both made the site feel alive and set the tone for the community on Reddit. They wanted Reddit to appeal to their peer group, which I take to mean that they wanted the site to appeal to a young, technologically-savvy crowd. Archives of Reddit during this time period confirms a heavy "techie" slant to the content.

In November 2005, Reddit merged with software

developer Aaron Swartz's company Infogami (which was a content management system for creating rich websites) after Infogami had failed to secure further funding. As a result of the negotiations, Swartz became an equal owner of Reddit's new parent company, Not A Bug, and was given the title of co-founder of Reddit despite joining onto the project six months after its start.

Commenting was added in December 2005, marking the first obvious development in Reddit's gradual shift towards becoming a social media site. Through the next few months into early 2006, most links would only garner a comment count in the single digits, indicating either that Reddit's user base was still quite small, or that users were initially mostly indifferent to the comment section feature.

The first subreddit was created on January 19, 2006. This was the /r/NSFW (Not Safe For Work) community, the purpose of which was to keep nudity and crude content off the home page of the site but to leave it accessible to users who still wished to see it. The next two communities created were /r/science and /r/programming, topics which further confirm my suspicions that Ohanian and Huffman were successful in attracting the type of audience that they had envisioned to Reddit. Through the heavy-handed manipulation of its founders, Reddit attracted an audience mainly consisting of programmers, engineers, scientists, and people in other technology-related fields. It shouldn't be controversial to claim that Reddit's initial user base likely had an above-average intelligence level. Research does indicate that people attracted to science and technology professions have higher IQs on average than the general population.[9]

So Reddit's culture was seeded by a bunch of smarter-than-average people, who likely *knew* that they were intelligent, posting pseudonymously. Did the desire to express and convey one's level of intelligence become a cultural norm of Reddit? I think so! Consider this quote from Reddit co-founder Alexis Ohanian regarding Reddit's culture: "Reddit is witty and sharp, and that applies to all aspects of the site, including responses to foolish comments and posts."[10]

I assert that users' desire to be seen as intelligent has been a core influence on the site's culture from the very beginning. A common accusation of Reddit users is that they love to argue, even more so than users of other internet sites. It's this mental sparring on a public stage (the comment section of a post) where Redditors can play out this intelligence contest. Even as the site's audience has broadened over the years, the desire to convey one's intelligence has been transmitted through social learning as new users observe and assimilate to Reddit's culture.

In October 2006, Not A Bug (and thus Reddit) was acquired by Condé Nast Publications; details of the deal were not public, although rumors at the time placed the purchase price in the realm of $10–20 million (Ohanian would later confirm the $10 million figure in a post to his Twitter account in November 2020). Swartz was unhappy with the new corporate office environment after the buyout, mentioning in a May 2007 interview with *Blogoscoped*, "I'd come in late and set up lots of off-site meetings and stuff. And my boss wasn't really thrilled about that." He also revealed that he had left Reddit a few months earlier upon being asked to resign.[11] Whether Swartz's newfound wealth (one-third of the buyout obviously made him a millionaire several times over) affected his attitude towards Reddit or if it was truly just a lifestyle conflict will remain unclear.

After the relationship with Swartz went sour, Huffman and Ohanian began publicly clarifying that he was technically a co-owner and not a co-founder of Reddit. Commenting as "AaronSw" on Reddit in May 2007, Swartz wrote, "One of the points of the merger was that we would all call ourselves co-founders, so that's what I've been doing. I'd be happy to stop if that's what Steve and Alexis wanted, though." Huffman and Ohanian both continued to work at Reddit until 2009, when they both departed on good terms to pursue other projects, though several years later both men would return to work at Reddit — Ohanian becoming executive chairman in 2014 and Huffman returning to serve as CEO in 2015.

I joined Reddit in 2010, so that marks the beginning of the time period when I can speak with personal experience about the site. I was seventeen years old with an interest in science and technology, and was about to head to college where I started off in a Doctor of Pharmacy program but dropped out of it after freshman year and switched to engineering, mainly because I wanted to think and solve problems, not just engage in rote memorization of facts. My younger self had a minor affectation for pseudointellectual tendencies, so I liked it when people knew that I was smart. Needless to say, I fit in perfectly on Reddit.

Some of the top communities on Reddit in late 2010 were /r/funny, /r/pics (pictures), /r/WTF, /r/science, /r/politics, /r/WorldNews, /r/AskReddit (a forum where users answer a question posed by the submitter), /r/gaming, /r/programming, and /r/technology. At the time, users signing up to Reddit would automatically be enrolled in a list of fifty "default" subscriptions curated by the site administrators for the purpose of enabling users "to discover the rich content that existed on the site." Users could choose to leave these communities and join additional ones, but for historical context it is important to recognize that these fifty communities — the list of which was altered slightly over the years — were reinforced as some of the largest and most active communities on Reddit due to new users automatically being subscribed to them. This practice of automatically subscribing new users to a list of default subreddits ended in 2017.

As I became more familiar with Reddit, I began unsubscribing from the default communities that I found dull or distasteful and slowly discovered ones which were more aligned to my interests, or even just began exploring topics that I figured I might have an interest in. I thought it was amazing how in many Reddit threads — more so the ones focused on science, a technical topic, or a particular hobby as opposed to the entertainment threads or memes — there seemed to be a few posters that were quite knowledgeable about the topic at hand discussing it in the comments. I certainly got the initial perception that Reddit was full of smart people who could write intelligently and at length about various subjects.

One cultural element that I recall very strongly from the Reddit of the early 2010s is something I mentioned earlier: the belief that Reddit is not a social media site. It was more than just that though, Redditors seemed to strongly agree that Reddit was *better* than Facebook and Twitter in nearly every way. That quote from Alexis Ohanian about Redditors being "witty and sharp," well that's truly the way in which moderate and heavy users of the site thought of themselves. Users who felt that the site was truly something special weren't just people who happened to browse Reddit — they identified as Redditors and felt a connection to the site's culture.

It isn't enough just to *think* highly of oneself on Reddit, though. Sure, writing intelligently about a topic was admired and garnered many upvotes. But conveying one's intelligence relative to other users by intellectually besting them was one of the main spectacles in the comment section of posts. The victor would be determined by the court of public opinion, garnering upvotes, while the loser would be "downvoted into oblivion," oftentimes choosing to delete their comments once the tide turned against them to protect their karma score from further bruising.

I'd certainly hesitate to call the manner in which most Reddit users engage with each other as debate. I view debate as a civil approach for comparing ideas and learning. If you're simply having a conversation with people who enjoy discussion, you don't need to win. What Redditors do is more like quarreling; a heated argument. Notice Ohanian's specific verbiage referring to how users engage with "foolish comments and posts." Arguing on Reddit isn't just about proving the merit of your ideas; above all, it's about proving that your opponent is a fool relative to yourself.

I'll admit that after observing this technique for a bit, I began to engage in it myself. I assimilated to the Reddit culture of argument out of a desire to also feel smart and prove my intelligence. So began the rabbit hole of years of evenings spent arguing with strangers on the internet. There's an implicit structure to many disagreements on Reddit that I was using myself when engaging with these users, but didn't even consciously recognize until I began to mature and take a step back from the site. Typically, a Redditor looking to one-up another user will reply in a specific format. They will quote various points from your comment with inline rebuttals using the site's Markdown comment syntax. There will likely be several insults peppered throughout to denigrate the opponent and demonstrate that they're simply a moron, while simultaneously attempting to prove that the commenter is the superior authority on the topic. Occasionally, linked sources will be provided, but in my experience these "sources" often do not even support the conclusion that the user claims they do. That doesn't matter, though, because the vast majority of readers of the comment section will not click on or parse the sources for accuracy, but instead be swayed by the *appearance* of a thoroughly constructed rebuttal.

Redditors frequently claim to love science, though what they actually love is their own misconception of science which provides them with a hearty dose of confirmation bias. By and large, most Redditors seem to have little understanding of the scientific method, and worship any scientific findings as objective truth when in reality this is a standard that scientific research aspires to but almost never attains. An observer will note that when discussing scientific topics, Redditors almost always link to "pop science" news articles — it is an important distinction to point out that these are written by journalists, not scientists — where the journalist interprets the findings of some study completed by actual scientists, then oversimplifies the results of the paper to present to a layman audience. Of course with the journalist as a mediator this nearly always results in any nuance, caveats, or uncertainty in the results being completely lost, and zero analysis as to the rigor or reproducibility of the study will be performed, allowing junk science to propagate heavily through these pop science channels. If Redditors truly loved science, the site would be filled with people linking to scientific journals rather than using news articles as their main ammunition when debating topics (that is, when they bother to provide a source for their claims at all). Not heading straight to the primary source indicates either an inability on the part of most Redditors to parse and understand scientific literature, or belies their true motivations to confirm their preexisting beliefs when debating such topics rather than arrive more closely at the truth even if it proves them personally wrong — which would certainly not be very scientific of them.

Remember, the objective of a disagreement on Reddit is often not to debate, openly exchange ideas, and educate. The objective is not even to convince one's opponent of their incorrectness relative to you, but rather to convince the broader voting community of this hierarchy. Clever personal attacks in the ad hominem style accomplish this in a crowd-pleasing dramatic fashion. Frequently it seems that the relative karma scores of two users arguing on Reddit are not based on the substance of their discussion, but rather who was able to more creatively and convincingly belittle his opponent's intelligence without simply resorting to crude profanity.

It's hard not to get sucked into participating in this behavior when it's so ingrained in the site's culture. Simply by leaving a comment on Reddit, you are inviting other users to reply to you. A user looking for an argument may engage with you in a hostile manner over something as silly as a semantic misunderstanding which then becomes their attack vector. If they reply in the above manner and you choose not to engage, the court of public opinion on Reddit will determine that you must have not replied because you were thoroughly blown out by their argument. To adolescents and young men especially, this attack on one's ego is hard to brush off. Moreover, the air of smug superiority that exudes from some users' replies can be infuriating, especially when they are engaging in an arrogant emotional outburst over something that they believe is true which can be disproven by multiple respectable sources after spending two minutes on an internet search engine.

The quality of discussion on Reddit took a major blow in January 2022 when site administrators rolled out updates to the user blocking feature. Previously, if User A blocked User B, User A would no longer see any posts, comments, or messages from User B (who retained the ability to reply to User A's content for *others* to see). This allowed Redditors to put anybody who was harassing them out of sight and out of mind. The new blocking updates were much more strict, though. Now if User A blocked User B, *neither* user would see each other's content, thus User B is now completely prohibited from replying to User A's content. This extended to comment chains as well, for example if User C replied to a comment by User A, User B could not reply to User C, or participate anywhere in the comment chain downstream of where User A participated.

This feature quickly began to be abused by those looking to argue in bad faith on Reddit. Argumentative people are generally obsessed with getting the last word, and this desire is paramount among Redditors. In online arguments, usually one party will eventually choose to stop participating rather than conceding, thus many Redditors with poor debate skills compensate for this with *endurance* rather than substance. When their opponent simply grows tired of wasting time interacting with them, such a user will declare that they've finally intellectually vanquished their opponent. The updated blocking feature made acquiring this hollow victory much easier, because in the face of the slightest dissent, a user could craft their reply and then immediately block their opponent, rendering them physically unable to participate any further in the discussion. To observers, it simply looked as though the intervening user was immediately "shut down" and could not even muster a retort.

User "ConversationCold8641" tested their ability to spread misinformation and propaganda with the new feature, and found that over the course of ten submissions where they would block every user that left a negative comment, their misinformation performed sequentially better. By targeting a community with this approach, the user was eventually able to boost misinformation to the top-ranking spot simply by rendering it invisible to the most active users that tended to call out propaganda. They were unable to see, vote on, or leave comments on any further submissions made by this user, demonstrating that a user could harness the updated blocking feature to create false consensus and further the issue of echo chambers on Reddit.

In September 2022, Reddit administrators said they were working on updates to prevent the blocking feature being used to restrict participation from entire comment chains, and would be testing a range of values such that a user who was blocked could participate within the second to fifteenth nested reply after the point where the user who had blocked them had commented. Several Redditors commented that the changes were tone-deaf and didn't fix the crux of the issue when the old blocking system worked ideally, with "Tyler1492" writing, "this assumption that everyone who [was] ever blocked was harassing the person blocking them is either extremely naïve or very dishonest." In the time since the blocking system was updated, seemingly hundreds of Redditors have submitted comments reporting their encounters with bad faith actors who gleefully abused the feature to permanently silence any direct replies from anybody who challenged them.

Obviously, not all users on Reddit engage with others in such a hostile manner. I can't recall a single time that I met a rude user in Reddit's /r/tea community, for example. In the over a decade I spent on the site, I maintained a "golden rule" policy. I was polite and respectful when interacting with other users up until the point where someone began to insult me, and then I would give it right back to them. In hindsight, this was still a complete waste of time and made me no better than them. But the sheer amount of arguments I was dragged into despite my solely retaliatory policy demonstrates how common it is for Reddit's users to engage with each other in a hostile, argumentative manner.

I've now spent quite a bit of time discussing a single aspect of Reddit's culture. And that's because I believe that Reddit users' desire to express and convey their own level of intelligence is by far the most negative aspect of the site's culture. But let's touch on a few other examples for a complete illustration of how interacting with Redditors is nothing like how a normal human might behave in a face-to-face interaction.

Reddit's culture also includes many idiosyncrasies, which

comparatively mostly just come off as banal irritations. Readers of comment sections on the site will often find comment threads full of pun-based jokes in reference to the subject of the parent post or in reply to another user's pun. If a Redditor references the lyrics to a song, you can guarantee that other users will come along and reply to each other by typing out the next line of the song. They engage in the same chain-reply concept with movie and television quotes; it's probable that every famous scene from visual media produced over the past several decades has at some point been completely re-typed by Redditors. Sometimes the comment replies on these types of threads will be nested dozens deep, to the point where you begin to wonder whether such users have ever heard of the concept of beating a dead horse.

Clichés and inside jokes also run rampant on Reddit, typically in reference to some post or comment that occurred previously in the site's history and became popular due to being funny or shocking. There is essentially an entire catalog of Reddit lore from the site's nearly two decades of existence, and users who are proud to identify as Redditors have a tendency to immerse themselves in it. Redditors relish the opportunity to link explanations of these references to other users who admit that they don't get it. These inside jokes are the type of thing that will maybe elicit a mild chuckle when you first join the site. After a while, one finds themselves questioning how the users participating in and upvoting these long-running phrases, references, and clichés don't find them utterly repetitive and completely stale.

That Redditors tend to parrot the same general comments over and over could not be more ironic when juxtaposed with the fact that many users hate "reposts," which is when a parent post submitted to a community has already been posted in the past and became popular. Whenever this happens, there will be a split opinion and debate among users in the comment section. Some Redditors will haughtily point out that the submission is a repost, and use third-party tools to identify and link each and every time the same image or GIF made it to the front page of the site, even if the most recent occurrence was several years ago. Other, more casual users of the site will reply that they hadn't seen the post before so it was new to *them*, and that they enjoyed seeing it. I point this out to demonstrate that to some hardcore Redditors, having an encyclopedic knowledge of every historical major event and popular post on the site is worn as a badge of honor, demonstrating their long tenure on the site, commitment to visiting daily, and how much value they place on immersion in Reddit's culture.

Many Redditors are so desperate to be seen as comedians that some comment sections on the site contain little other than an endless deluge of their attempts at making jokes. In 2013, the moderators of /r/AskReddit attempted to stymie this by allowing users submitting questions to the subreddit to choose to put a "serious" tag on their post. Their decision explains, "in threads that are tagged as serious, the moderators will make an effort to remove any joke answers or off-topic comments." After the introduction of this feature, several users noted that the amount of comments that "serious" threads received was small relative to threads with no restrictions, indicating that many Redditors had nothing at all to add to these discussions when they were unable to resort to puns, pop culture references, and regurgitated inside jokes. Personally, I recall this decision being a welcome respite from /r/AskReddit threads which were at the time filled with the "tree fiddy" meme, a reference to a 1999 South Park episode wherein Redditors would construct elaborate, seemingly real stories in response to a poster's query only for the story to reveal itself as a bait-and-switch near the end, featuring an appearance by the Loch Ness Monster begging for three dollars and fifty cents.

In my experience, one can avoid most of these irritating minor quirks of Redditors by staying out of the site's largest communities, indicating that these performative behaviors are likely done for karma points more so than a sense of belongingness. By contrast, ego and behavioral psychology fuel the heated arguments which regularly occur on Reddit. These quarrels are a manifestation of what I believe is a deep-seated cultural norm on the site, the desire to convey one's intelligence. As I have demonstrated, this can likely be traced all the way back to the founding of the site in 2005 via the near total control that Alexis Ohanian and Steve Huffman had to shape the website in their vision. At this point it has permeated the site nearly completely; there are very few communities left on Reddit where one can exchange and debate facts, thoughts, and ideas in a civil manner.

Chapter 5
The Pseudonymity Dilemma

For many years, a debate has been raging regarding the value of anonymity on the internet. On one side are those who argue that online anonymity is vitally important to freedom of expression on the internet. Facing off against them are champions of the "Real Name Web," who would counter that verified identities are an essential prerequisite to having authentic interactions online.

Of course, nearly no philosophical issue is as one-sided as the highly polarized proponents on either end of the spectrum would have you believe. In all practicality, though, those who argue for a fully anonymous internet have already lost. The very structure of how we access the web today through Internet Service Providers as gatekeepers means that true anonymity is impossible. Tools like Virtual Private Networks can shift trust around, but there is no guaranteed solution to remaining anonymous on the internet — other than staying off of it completely.

As such, the best that privacy-focused web denizens can achieve under the current system is pseudo-anonymity and pseudonymity. The terms are similar phonetically, but the distinction is important. Pseudo-anonymity is the false appearance of anonymity — for example, users on the site 4chan by default all submit comments under the moniker "anonymous." Users generally have no continuity of identity from one comment or thread to the next. However, site administrators have access to IP addresses and other logged information which could allow them to identify users such that they are not *truly* anonymous. Due to the aforementioned impossibility of achieving true anonymity on the internet, pseudo-anonymity is the best possible case for essentially all online activities.

Pseudonymity is the act of identifying oneself using a fake name, a pseudonym. On the internet this tactic has been employed since the days of the earliest message boards, and throughout history written works have been created under pseudonyms to mask the true identity of the author. The motivations were varying, such as not wanting to be held personally responsible for controversial writings, or desiring a piece to stand on its own merits rather than being judged by the preceding reputation of an author. Today, Reddit is one of many pseudonymous social websites where users can create their own unique screen names, effectively allowing them to build an entire online persona that is separate from their real identity.

Pseudonymity enables numerous benefits. Users can hide their real identity from other regular users by controlling exactly how much personal information they choose to share about themselves, such as their age, location, career, or other identifying characteristics. Freedom of speech can be exercised to a fuller extent when users are able to express controversial or minority opinions without fear of tangible retribution in the real world. Users may be more willing to help others by discussing personal or stigmatized topics such as medical conditions which they would not otherwise want revealed about themselves in the public record. This increased tendency towards self-disclosure on the internet is one facet of the "online disinhibition effect," a term coined by psychologist John Suler.[12]

On a personal level, privacy was a key consideration for me when starting my blog where I write about personal finance, investing, and my progress towards my goal of financial independence. To build credibility among my readers — something that I found sorely lacking in other money-related blogs — I decided to open my financial life up. I regularly share my income, net worth, and breakdowns of my spending. I didn't necessarily want coworkers or even most friends and family to be able to peer into my entire financial life by searching my name on Google, so I simply author articles under a pseudonym. If I had to post under my real identity, I probably would not have taken that first step towards writing about personal finance.

Unequivocally, the benefits of internet users being able to maintain a reasonable degree of anonymity are immense. Anybody who supports governments and especially corporations eroding these protections because they "have nothing to hide" is either speaking from a place of disingenuity or is taking the freedoms that they enjoy for granted. That being said, there are some significant and glaring drawbacks to anonymity on the web. I believe these are in no way large enough to make the "Real Name Web" a preferable solution, however they are absolutely worth keeping in mind when consuming content and interacting with other users on sites like Reddit.

The most obvious drawback of pseudonymity is that users have no way to vet each other as reliable sources of information or a person worthy of an investment of one's time to engage with. For all one knows, the person behind any given comment could either be a subject-matter expert, just some random teenager, a troll looking to make people angry or waste their time, or a subversive agent looking to promote a particular agenda. Users' profiles and comment histories can be investigated, however on top of requiring an investment of one's time, this will usually only ferret out the most inexperienced and low-effort trolls, as anybody skilled at that craft puts effort into evading easy detection.

Pathological liars and people in desperate need of validating their opinions at any cost would of course be particularly attracted to a pseudonymous environment. A person with a slick enough tongue and some adept Google-fu could craft a fake persona that is highly convincing to the vast majority of readers. Such people would be caught out and quickly stumble in a face-to-face conversation, however one can take as long as they like to write, research, and edit comments on the internet. In my time on Reddit I came across a few of these abject liars. I would read a comment or post and pick up on some inconsistency or incorrect fact that made me doubt the whole thing, then click on the user's profile to investigate. Oftentimes, it was just some silly teenager making stuff up for karma points. But sometimes I would find these strange profiles that were mired in detailed lies; the user was a surgeon today while last week they claimed to be a physicist; profiles where the user had posted several months apart wherein they had claimed to be completely different ages, genders, nationalities, or some other conflicting trait. Thankfully these users were few and far between, but in all cases they seemed to be very heavy users of Reddit.

Far more common on Reddit was what I termed the "experience exaggerator." These users wanted to be seen as authorities on topics which they had shallow depths of knowledge in, so they would inflate their credentials. For example, one that I noticed frequently was that users would begin a comment with an appeal to authority like "as an engineer," but upon digging into their profile I would discover that they were actually only a sophomore in college pursuing an engineering degree. I realized the irony that as a teenager and early-twenty-something I had myself spent countless hours spewing my uninformed, half-baked opinions all over Reddit as if they were immutable gospel. It was an eye-opening revelation when I finally understood that the demographics of other users on the internet had not aged in lockstep with myself, and that even as I grew more mature and informed there was an ever-replenishing supply of ignorant teenagers and young adults who were all too happy to take up the other side of a discussion on the internet about a topic they knew far less about than what could be gleaned from its Wikipedia entry.

The other side of the online disinhibition effect is that it can amplify negative behaviors as well, which Suler refers to as "toxic disinhibition." Some users may use the protection of pseudonymity to act more abusively towards others than they would in a face-to-face conversation or on a platform linked to their real name. We are more likely to stoop to hurling insults and vitriol at others online when our true identities are not attached to our words, and there is no risk of harm to one's real world physical self or reputation. If you are careful with how much personal information that you share online, other users will be completely unable to discover your true identity. Toxic disinhibition explains in part why it sometimes seems that we encounter jerks in nearly every online space at a much higher rate than when interacting with people in our daily lives. There's certainly the additional contributing factor that miserable losers are more likely to spend all day online, however it's also likely that some of your coworkers, friends, and family members who you otherwise know as perfectly pleasant people are Jekyll and Hydes who go home and act hostilely on the internet.

Some psychologists are quick to claim that everyone who

acts like a troll online is doing so because they're simply psychopaths or sadists who do it for the thrill of hurting others. Several studies on negative online behaviors torpedo their own credibility by utterly failing to distinguish that there are likely massive differences between the motivations of teenage girls cyberbullying people whom they personally know on social media, versus those of people logging onto pseudonymous sites where they instigate conflict and arguments or attempt to upset or annoy complete and total strangers whom they will likely never interact with again. I have always strongly felt that many otherwise normal, well-adjusted people can be easily swayed by the toxic disinhibition effect to engage in online trolling. A joint research paper out of Cornell and Stanford Universities titled "Anyone Can Become A Troll" corroborates this; the researchers found that the two primary factors influencing one's likelihood of engaging in trolling behavior were their mood and the context of existing discussion. They report that an individual being in a negative mood while encountering the trolling posts of other users doubled the participants' baseline rate of engaging in trolling themselves. While they found that past trolling behavior was predictive of future trolling, "mood and discussion context together can explain trolling behavior better than an individual's history of trolling. These results combine to suggest that ordinary people can, under the right circumstances, behave like trolls."[13]

I would indeed find that when I took the time to examine the post history of someone being a jerk online to myself or another user, they often had a comment history which included a fair amount of neutral and positive comments. While some users had comment histories filled with nothing but pages of vitriol and rage, those were rare, and it seemed to me that most users who engaged in toxicity online weren't *always* behaving like trolls. More likely they'd get into the occasional disagreement, and I even found a few users who heavily trolled only a single community on Reddit while acting perfectly reasonable in their interactions everywhere else on the site. I will admit to trolling other Redditors in response to some rude behavior or insults that they levied my way, and in the decade-plus that I spent on the site I verbally eviscerated two or three users so thoroughly that they deleted their accounts on the site entirely. In hindsight, most of the arguments that I got into on Reddit via my retaliatory policy were probably just with normal people (that is, not sadists or psychopaths) who were having a bad day and looking to vent some negative emotions in a low-consequence manner, and whatever comment they scrolled past that they disagreed with was good enough for that purpose. The negative context of their reply and the attack on my ego of course meant that I felt that I had to respond with escalating force fueled by righteous anger — which, even if one would argue is justified in that circumstance, is still an utter waste of one's time.

There are definitely some genuinely awful people out there whose main motivation for going online is to make others miserable, but I believe if you took a sum total of all the arguments that occur in a single day on Reddit, such people would not account for anywhere near the majority of them. While it is interesting to examine why people are motivated to act negatively online and who might be behind the screen typing such comments, knowing this information does not change that these interactions will still occur. Simply reading Reddit threads will expose you to toxicity regularly, and actively posting on the site opens the door for toxicity to be directed at you, sometimes for no reason at all. You don't *have* to respond, but you probably did at least read it, and for some trolls that knowledge is enough of a victory.

The main drawback of pseudonymity when it comes to motivated trolls is that they cannot be dealt with effectively or permanently. Creating a new account on Reddit is instant and free, hence any user banned from a particular community or from Reddit as a whole will not be banned for long. Evading IP bans or browser fingerprinting is child's play for those with minor computer literacy skills. I was once a subreddit moderator for a short while, and what seemed to be the same two or three people (based on similarities in linguistic patterns and post content) would come back day after day on new accounts after being banned in order to harass users of the community. The Reddit administrators were no help, but what could they do? It's not like users are required to verify their identity before registering for a Reddit account. It's a necessary byproduct of a pseudonymous system that permanently banning trolls and problematic users is impossible. Many consider that a worthy price to pay in exchange for maintaining most of their privacy online.

Finally, we want to consider that as artificial intelligence and natural language processing continue to advance, at some point in the near future it will become increasingly hard to distinguish whether we are interacting with other humans or with bots. In fact, we may already be rapidly approaching that point. In late 2020, a bot powered by OpenAI's GPT-3 language model which uses deep learning to produce human-like text posted on Reddit's /r/AskReddit forum for a week before the account was identified as a bot. Software engineer Philip Winston was the first to publicly out the bot on his blog.[14] A few Reddit users had previously replied to the GPT-3 bot's comments and accused it of being a bot, but many more Redditors were interacting with it as if it was a human.

There were some comments which had tells that they were written by a bot, though many were flawless imitations of human speech. However, the main thing that gave it away was the bot responding to posts within seconds, and writing long-form posts at a frequency of once per minute. If the commenting frequency were toned down and the length of the posts reduced such that they were less complex, the GPT-3 bot would likely have gone much longer before being detected.

In his blog post outing the bot, Winston notes that the quality of its writing would have been impossible a few short years ago, and obviously these language models will only continue to improve going forward. He then asks questions which none of us have answers to yet: "Given this progress, how will we tell AI-generated text from human-generated text? It seems clear that will become increasingly impossible. What happens to social networks at that point, what happens to the entire internet, what happens to us?"

Chapter 6

The (Former) Front Page of the Internet

Reddit's longest-running slogan saw its demise in July 2021. No longer would the site tagline populate users' browser tab field with the self-proclamation of being "the front page of the internet," a claim which it had maintained for just over a decade since June 2011. To long-time users of Reddit who felt that the site had overall been slowly changing for the worse, this was just one more small indication that the Reddit they were using today was no longer the same website that they fell in love with many years ago.

A brief history of Reddit's many slogans begins with the site's launch in June 2005, when the tagline was "Reddit - what's new online." This original statement was perfectly descriptive of the site's original purpose as an online news link aggregator. The original motto stuck around until September 2010, when it was changed to "where dreams come true," a humorous suggestion by one user following Reddit's success in inspiring paradoxical politicizers Jon Stewart and Stephen Colbert to create their own rallies satirizing an earlier one put on by Glenn Beck.

Jokes like that quickly grow stale though, and just a month later in October 2010 Reddit again swapped their tagline, this time to "the voice of the internet – news before it happens." The latter part of the slogan harkened back to Reddit's original tagline and purpose as a speedy link aggregator. The first half was a nod to the site's development into a discussion platform that in just five years had become one of the most popular hangouts on the web and a driving force in shaping online culture. For some reason, this tagline did not even last a full year; perhaps it just lacked the clever conciseness that webmasters aim for.

In June 2011, the slogan that stuck with Reddit during nearly my entire tenure on the site was unveiled. "Reddit: the front page of the internet." It was succinct; it reflected the fact that content on the site had expanded far beyond just news; it hinted at the site's increasingly influential and preeminent role among online spaces without being overly aggrandizing. Perhaps Reddit wanted a tagline that they could grow into.

Social criticisms of Reddit's overall community sometimes brought the accuracy of the tagline under fire. A 2017 article written by Samantha Allen in *The Daily Beast* opens, "Reddit is not 'the front page of the Internet,' as its slogan proclaims. The site is a massive generator of web traffic but, in demographic terms, Reddit might more aptly be called the front page of a very *specific* Internet, a mostly young and mostly male Internet." Allen's article notes that only six percent of online adults visited Reddit in 2017.[15] It was probably more apt to state that the tagline reflected what Reddit was to its users rather than to denizens of the internet as a whole.

To zero fanfare or explanation by site administrators, Reddit voluntarily uncrowned itself as "the front page of the internet" in July 2021. The new tagline would be "dive into anything," perhaps instead trying to sell a more humble angle that encouraged visitors to explore the site's countless niche communities. Several threads popped up in various subreddits with users reacting to and questioning the unannounced change. Quite a few commenters said that they had not even noticed the change until it was pointed out to them (which makes sense when acknowledging that many Redditors nowadays access the site solely through a smartphone app and not a desktop or even mobile web browser).

Users' reactions to the death of the site's most enduring tagline were primarily negative. The most highly upvoted comment in one of these threads was a user sardonically joking that "'step in something unpleasant' seems more appropriate for Reddit these days." Another user proposed, "How about 'Internet Reruns' instead? It's all just the same posts and comments over and over." Redditors who chimed in overwhelmingly agreed that they liked the previous slogan better. Were they just resistant to change, or did the demise of "the front page of the internet" represent something more to them, symbolically shattering their idea of what they thought that Reddit was, and confirming their feelings that the site had been changing for the worse over the years?

Perhaps the rebranding was for the best, though. The internet is at once both a vast expanse, and a relatively consolidated empire wherein most users exist in a small bubble, mainly on their preferred social media platform of choice. Each of these platforms tend to have their own unique cultures and demographic quirks. Any fantasies that Reddit users or Reddit, Incorporated had about the site being the definitive cultural wellspring for the entire internet were a product of Reddit's insular culture and unfulfilled wishful thinking from the first half of the 2010s.

It's simple logic that Reddit cannot be the front page of the internet unless it is the most visited site online, with proportional representation from each demographic on the internet as a whole. The content in Reddit's /r/all and /r/popular feeds represents what users in the Reddit bubble want to see, not what the median internet user wants to see. Let's take a look at what type of content we can find on /r/all. For context, /r/all is described as "a less filtered feed of the most popular posts on Reddit. When you're on /r/all, sexually explicit posts are filtered out but other popular Not Safe for Work (NSFW) posts are included."

The below is a complete bulleted list of the top twenty-five posts on Reddit's /r/all feed, observed on a weekday morning in May 2022 around 9:30 AM EDT (there is no particular importance to this date other than that it happened to be when I began drafting this chapter):

- 9 image posts
  - 2 images which are supposed to be humorous references to pop culture media (one related to Marvel superhero movies and the other a children's television cartoon)
  - 2 images stoking outrage/mocking over the actions of others
  - 2 images which are supposed to be some degree of "interesting"
  - 1 meta (self-referential) meme poking fun at Reddit users
  - 1 image used to deliver a joke about British people
  - 1 comic related to global news events, which is supposed to be humorous
- 7 GIFs (animations)
  - 3 GIFs which are supposed to be funny
  - 2 GIFs featuring gameplay of a video game
  - 1 GIF related to nature and animals
  - 1 GIF related to sports

- 6 screenshots of social media sites
  - 3 screenshots of Twitter posts (one each topic: humor, politics, celebrity gossip)
  - 1 screenshot of a user's comment replying to an /r/AskReddit post (topic: humor)
  - 1 screenshot of a user's comment on a Reddit post which *itself* is a screenshot of a Twitter post (topic: politics/outrage)
  - 1 screenshot of a 4chan post (topic: humor)
- 1 article relating to global news events
- 1 video relating to global news events
- 1 thread polling the users of a specific community

My first takeaway is that images comprise nearly all of the most popular posts on Reddit, followed by GIFs. This is in stark contrast to the earliest days of Reddit, when the site was exclusively an aggregator of links to articles and other websites. I only found one single article in the top twenty-five most popular posts on /r/all that morning.

Next, I was surprised by the number of posts on /r/all which are simply screenshots from various social media sites, especially Twitter. To verify that this wasn't an outlier, I went back to /r/all on random days over the following few months, and I confirmed that at any given time, roughly a quarter of the posts on /r/all are screenshots from other social media sites, most commonly Twitter. Usually these screenshots seem to be related to politics, social issues, or an attempt at humor. Perhaps the reason that Twitter posts perform so well on Reddit is that tweets are forced to be succinct, and this indisputably easily-digestible content simply performs well when placed in echo chamber communities on Reddit where users already agree with the tweet's premise thus providing them with confirmation bias.

Clearly, numerous posts on /r/all are trying to be funny (satisfying my earlier assertion that Redditors thinking of themselves as comedians is a facet of the site's culture), but I honestly haven't found very many of them humorous. Most of the "jokes" are immature, self-deprecating, or a desperate grab at dark and edgy humor that is overly reliant on shock value. I am barely clinging onto the tail-end of Reddit's largest demographic of eighteen- to twenty-nine-year-olds, and I have a hard time trying to figure out how enough people are upvoting this crap to consistently get it to the front page. A few times in my life I have been in the physical presence of avid Redditors who shared the site's sense of humor, and nearly everything they said was received by others with a blank stare or extremely forced, polite chuckles.

Redditors absolutely love science fiction and fantasy media franchises. News, memes, references, and inside jokes related to Star Wars, The Lord of the Rings, superhero movies, and the children's cartoon Avatar: The Last Airbender frequently make it into the most popular posts on /r/all. Several subreddits related to these franchises exist on Reddit, and the content generated by them is apparently agreeable enough with a large swath of Reddit users that at least one of these franchises nearly always has some presence on the front page. Users who are not superfans of these particular sci-fi and fantasy movies and television shows will find themselves frequently out of the loop, and likely consider Reddit's utter obsession with them strange, and perhaps indicative of questionable taste in some cases. Celebrity news and gossip almost never makes it to /r/all — in fact, the act of celebrity worship tends to be actively derided by many Redditors — *unless* it relates to the actors, actresses, or writers of one of the aforementioned franchises, in which case such gossip is more than acceptable, and the comment section will be filled with users fawning over the celebrity. Instances of such self-contradiction and blind hypocrisy are rather common in the behavior of Redditors.

Despite seeing worldwide traffic, Reddit is a heavily Americentric website. According to a May 2022 survey by *Statista*, nearly half (forty-seven percent) of desktop traffic to Reddit was from the United States. This was a factor of over six times larger than the next most common traffic source, which was from the United Kingdom at approximately seven and a half percent of desktop traffic to Reddit.[16] Consequentially, news and political topics which are represented on /r/all tend to be from an American perspective. Furthermore, the most popular political content on Reddit leans heavily leftward.

Even though Reddit has certainly expanded its demographic reach slightly since Samantha Allen's 2017 article, her criticism that Reddit is "the front page of a very *specific* Internet" is still apt. The most popular posts on Reddit clearly reflect the tastes of an audience which is overwhelmingly comprised of teenagers and young adult American males who are politically left-leaning and have an interest in aspects of geek culture. There's nothing wrong with that group settling on Reddit per se, but in giving up "the front page of the internet" moniker, it seems that Reddit has finally accepted that this demographic is one that does not and can not speak for internet users as a whole.

It is not difficult to find vocal Redditors who express the sentiment that they don't browse /r/all or /r/popular due to disliking the content posted there for a myriad of reasons. Some users have an additional self-imposed rule that they simply stay away from the site's largest subreddits, perceiving an inverse relationship between the number of users subscribed to a community and the quality of the content and discussion within. In my experience this is generally accurate — one cannot get a complete taste of Reddit's culture without venturing into the largest subreddits as it is there where users' incentives to engage in their characteristic performative behaviors in exchange for karma points will necessarily be the greatest. Users who have signed up for a Reddit account can join and leave subreddits at will, curating their own front page of Reddit and never seeing the /r/all or /r/popular feeds unless they explicitly choose to click on them.

There exists a group of cloistered Redditors who spend all of their time on the site in niche communities dedicated to their interests, lifestyle, and hobbies which are simply too small to have any posts make it into the /r/all feed. Their primary motive is to curate a higher quality online experience for themselves that is more interesting and entertaining, and — tucked away from the masses of Redditors — perhaps even a bit more peaceful. This curation approach was how I used Reddit for the majority of my tenure on the site, as I found Reddit's culture irritating and most of the posts on /r/all and /r/popular to be uninteresting or distasteful. Does this methodology reveal the path to an idyllic Reddit experience, or was I simply fooling myself for all of those years?

Chapter 7
Curating Cope: The Knowledge Subreddit Fallacy

When I accuse Reddit of being filled with low-value content, many people seem to assume that I must be referring only to the /r/popular and /r/all feeds, the contents of which we examined in the prior chapter. Perhaps the most common defense that I hear is from people who think that *their* curated list of subreddit subscriptions is an exception. However, these niche communities providing a superior experience to the largest subreddits is a very low bar, and does not necessarily mean that they cross the threshold of being worth using.

We first need to dig past the layers of unfunny memes, pop culture garbage, videos, and social media screenshots that dominate Reddit's largest communities and which comprise almost all the content on the /r/all and /r/popular feeds. Let's call these "entertainment subreddits." Once we've filtered out these largest communities, we find a thriving ecosystem of smaller subreddits that focus on hobbies, professions, and lifestyle content. Some example communities that I've used in the past that fit this bill would be things like /r/investing, /r/engineering, /r/minimalism, /r/tea, /r/guitar, and countless others. I'm going to call these "knowledge subreddits" because people participate in communities like these for two main reasons:

1. To learn more about topics they are involved in (or tentatively exploring) and expand their knowledge base; mostly by reading, occasionally by asking questions, and by keeping track of new developments.
2. To share their amassed knowledge with others on topics that they are passionate about.

Unfortunately, I have come to realize that these knowledge subreddits are no exception: they are also incredibly low-value. Value in this case I would define as the accuracy of the information and depth or quality of discussion, which I feel is a fair yardstick given the motivations for use presented above, as well as the fact that many users of such communities often use them to justify their time spent on Reddit as being educational or productive.

As we've already discussed, Reddit is just one big conversation with a bunch of pseudonymous users. You don't know anybody's credentials, and you can never completely believe that someone has any qualifications that they may claim to. The biggest issue with these knowledge subreddits is that users have no way to vet the information presented therein, unless they are *already* an expert in that topic! This clearly presents a catch-22.

Are you an expert in anything? Not from reading about it on Reddit, but do you have something that you have spent thousands of hours educating yourself on from a diverse collection of sources, practicing, refining, and discussing with other (verified) experts in that topic? Do you have a degree in any field? Would someone pay you to apply this knowledge? That's okay if you aren't an expert in anything yet — maybe like me, you wasted most of your free time for years and years browsing time-wasting websites instead of pursuing more intentional activities. After finishing Part II of this book and changing your internet habits, you could be well on your way to becoming an expert in whatever topic you desire in likely just a few short years.

But if you are an expert in something, anything, I want you to put down this book and perform an exercise. Find the main community on Reddit dedicated to that topic in which you are an expert. Set a timer for ten minutes, and when it goes off, you *must* close Reddit and return here. I want you to take a piece of paper with a writing utensil, and go read the comments on several different popular discussions in that community. When either of the following occurs, add a tick mark to your paper:

1. A user whose comment is factually incorrect, logically flawed, or a gross oversimplification has been upvoted by the community.
2. A user whose comment is completely factually correct was downvoted by the community.

Done? You almost certainly have at least one tick mark on your paper, and likely several. Now extrapolate the rate at which you encountered misinformation over an hour or two of browsing that community. In fact, you will find that when you go to any subreddit focused on a topic that you are knowledgeable or an expert in, you will notice that a fair bit of what the Redditors in that community are regurgitating is wrong.

The most important takeaway from this chapter is to realize that this level of bullshitting on Reddit isn't just exclusive to the community surrounding your topic(s) of expertise. Every knowledge subreddit is like that, but we simply lack the tools to immediately identify misinformation that we read regarding the vast variety of other topics in which we are *not* experts.

I propose that due to several influencing factors, essentially every subreddit community stagnates at a low level of knowledge. The structure of Reddit and the behavior of its users causes these communities to become stuck as echo chambers appealing to the lowest common denominator, which is the knowledge level of a complete beginner.

In a previous chapter, we discussed the flaws of Reddit's karma system and how people upvoting information they agree with and downvoting information that they disagree with contributes to forming echo chambers on Reddit. Whatever conforms to the existing beliefs of the majority of voting users will get more exposure, while content that contradicts their existing beliefs — even if factually correct — will tend to be downvoted and hidden. We've also discussed illusory superiority and the cultural norm of argument and one-upmanship on Reddit. Oftentimes, this combination will lead to users who bring contradictory information to the existing group beliefs not only collecting downvotes, but also being verbally attacked by members of the community.

It's easy to see how these forces coalesce into keeping these knowledge subreddits at a low level of information. What I have observed is that general assumptions which are true *most* of the time are relentlessly parroted in these communities as if they were unyielding gospel. For example, in science subreddits, the most highly-upvoted posts and comments tend to be simplistic explanations incorporating well-known "pop science," that is, concepts that have been dumbed down for a general audience and are presented with factual authority as compared to actual scientific discussion which tends to make heavy use of qualifiers and almost never presents any finding with complete certainty. Users who actually understand the field being discussed who take the time to write lengthy, well-sourced comments adhering to scientific integrity will commonly find that their post is almost completely ignored in favor of the oversimplified, partially-incorrect pop science explanations.

Education on a given topic does not stop at the beginner level, however it does for the vast majority of Reddit communities. Worse yet, I got the feeling that some percentage of the most active users in these communities seemed to have exclusively "educated" themselves on the topic at hand by reading other Reddit posts and comments. It's like a big game of telephone, with users endlessly repeating what they have "learned" from reading other Reddit comments in the same community. Somewhere along the learning spectrum towards achieving expertise on a topic is recognizing when those general assumptions that you learned as a beginner do not hold true, understanding why that is the case, and being able to cogently articulate an alternate conclusion.

On Reddit, pointing out these fringe exceptions to the common wisdom will often earn you downvotes and attract a horde of low-information users to insult and argue with you. I had this happen more and more frequently to me over the years as I gained knowledge and experience in various topics of interest to me. For example, I had a reasonably decent understanding of personal finance and investing by my late 20s due to thousands of hours spent reading the thoughts of verifiable experts in these fields, implementing that knowledge in my own life, and later even writing some articles of my own about related topics.

When I posted about these subjects, it was to share my knowledge with others and hopefully learn something new myself. When I replied to someone whose comment was incorrect, it was with the motivation that observers reading the thread would not be misled into acting on bad information rather than to chastise the user who had posted it, especially when it came to topics as important as managing one's life savings. I never engaged with users in the typical Reddit fashion — with the intention of making them look dumber than me — until that user had fired the first volley by insulting me in their reply. Still, the simple act of trying to share knowledge in a polite, conversational manner had a high chance of attracting rude, uninformed users to argue with me like flies to hot garbage. To many Redditors, it seems there is no higher insult than being told that they are incorrect, regardless of how tactfully it is delivered. This may partially explain why a user who disagrees with another often includes disparaging comments in their very first interaction; they likely share in the opinion that they've already levied the worst possible insult simply by insinuating that the person they are replying to is wrong, so they may as well add extra brunt to their retort.

I would occasionally lend moral support to other users who offered expert-level takes, but whose comments I found sitting in negative karma territory, with several users already circling around the wagon to tell them how stupid and wrong they were. I let them know that I appreciated their input, and how ludicrous it was that they were placed under fire because their knowledge disagreed with the hive mind. Usually I ate some negative karma points for my show of support. If they replied, it would usually be something along the lines of "yeah, Reddit sucks" or "I really need to quit posting here."

One complaint I recall was from an airline pilot sharing his or her experience answering other users' questions about air travel. The pilot was lamenting how often their expertise would be rejected, and they would be downvoted in favor of a user who had insulted them and then copied and pasted some basic, out-of-context information from a search engine to "prove" them wrong. The pilot expounded with one case where they investigated the post history of a user who they had this experience with, discovering that the user was a teenager. Yet because the teenager had been more adept at insulting the pilot with a clever quip in the fashion of a typical Reddit argument, as well as presenting information which intuitively felt correct to observers who were not experts in this particular field (despite it being wrong in this context), the teenager's comment won out.

It's this loss of nuance where the common knowledge falls short — better yet, the *active rejection* of it by the hive mind of most Reddit communities via attacking experts — that causes these knowledge subreddits to stagnate at a low level of information. It's a vicious cycle.

What follows is no surprise, which is that the experts are driven away from many of these communities. Knowledgeable people posting on the internet are already choosing to give away their time for free to educate others, usually only for the satisfaction of sharing their passion. A toxic environment like that provided by Reddit and other social media platforms only tilts the equation that much further towards this proposition not being worth it. One would need the patience and discipline of a monk to not let their mood be sullied by the rude and insulting way in which many Redditors treat other users.

Why continue to share access to one's time, attention, and thoughts for free to such unappreciative strangers? The expert could be doing anything else with that time: creating a blog or vlog where they own and profit from their own content, spending more time with family and friends, writing a book, simply spending their time *doing* activities related to their passion rather than talking about it, or even trying out a new hobby. These all end up being much more rewarding and satisfying activities than wading through a mire of vitriol on the internet to occasionally receive the thanks of an anonymous stranger who found your comment helpful.

I hung onto continuing to use Reddit for several years after identifying parts of this cycle. I foolishly believed that by continuing to spend my time providing correct, properly-sourced information in these communities that I could educate enough users to create a butterfly effect that would eventually fix some of the most vexing misconceptions that these communities held. It also let me avoid confronting my addiction to Reddit. Even though I knew I was getting little value out of the site, I could weakly justify my insane hours of usage by claiming I was doing a service for the communities surrounding my passions and interests.

In the end I was unable to affect any meaningful change, and if anything many of the subreddits that I followed got worse over time in terms of the quality of information and discussion contained therein as they continued to grow larger. This is likely due to the fact that many users just subscribe to communities that they have a tangential interest in learning about as they randomly stumble across them, whereas most of the experts would have already been there wanting to discuss the topic even when the community was small. Once a post from a community gets to the /r/all or /r/popular feeds and creates widespread awareness of the existence of a subreddit among the site's lowest-quality users who browse those feeds, the dilution of knowledge accelerates at a ridiculous rate. /r/FinancialIndependence, for example, went from a place where people were frequently having high-level investment portfolio modeling discussions and sharing research papers, to a place filled with beginners asking the same twenty basic questions and shouting down people with PhD-level knowledge who tried to tell them that the "rules" they'd read in articles on *Forbes* and *MSN Money* were just general guidelines and that financial modeling required more than basic algebra. That was the decline I observed in the level of discussion when the community started in 2011 compared to around when it passed 200,000 subscribers in 2017, so I can only imagine how much worse it is with that subreddit on track to surpass two million members in 2023.

After thousands of wasted hours on Reddit, I too decided to throw in the towel on sharing any knowledge on the site. Breaking my compulsion to continue *browsing* Reddit after over a decade of near-daily use was another matter which we will discuss in the second part of this book. But I would say that this decision to stop making effortful contributions to Reddit marked the true beginning of my journey to live more intentionally, and — once I got a taste of the reward and satisfaction inherent to more enriching hobbies — the start of my struggle to break away from time-wasting websites for good.

This was around July 2019, which I know because that is when I started my blog. I figured out that part of my desire to use Reddit was as an outlet to share my passion for personal finance, investing, and financial independence through writing. A blog, I reasoned, would fill that same desire and thus help me cut down on my Reddit usage, while also giving me a tangible product of achievement to point to.

By creating my own blog, I now fully owned my content and the ability to monetize it if my blog became popular. I controlled my own platform, where I could remove rude comments and ban any repeat offenders if needed. No longer would Reddit, Incorporated get to profit from my mental efforts for free. That taste of the satisfaction of actually *creating* something led to a positive feedback loop wherein I began to naturally find activities like browsing Reddit or playing video games gradually more unfulfilling.

When it came to my content *consumption* I found far more enriching, valuable sources of information once I started to break away from my zombie-like habit of scrolling through comments in Reddit communities related to my interests. I started reading books again after not touching one since finishing high school (which, not coincidentally, is around the time that I discovered Reddit). I sought out small, independent blogs run by knowledgeable authors who shared high-quality information. Additionally, I picked up some podcasts related to economics, whose hosts could expound more eloquently on the topic than any Reddit user I had encountered.

In his groundbreaking book *Digital Minimalism*, Cal Newport writes that when determining which sources to give our attention to, they should be people who have "proved to you to be reliably smart and insightful with their writing." As I began the long process of re-vectoring some of the time that I was spending consuming content towards these higher value alternatives, I also began to evaluate the habits of the people behind creating these books, blogs, and podcasts to see if there was something that I might learn as a budding writer myself.

Notably, the vast majority of these writers creating intelligent, insightful content that I admired seemed to have either a minuscule or nonexistent social media presence. If they did have social media accounts, in most cases it was a Twitter account where nearly all of their posts would be quick, simple updates announcing a new article or podcast episode. They were using social media as an advertisement tool and little more. If I wanted to receive their thoughts and ideas, I had to go to *their* platforms.

Ultimately, I concluded that there is no reason for anybody with anything worth saying to be on Reddit. Have you ever heard somebody who you consider to be an authority on *any* topic mention that they spend their time commenting on Reddit to share knowledge? Any possible virtues of discussing ideas are smothered by the massive downsides of the site and its users. There's no incentive for experts to fight the uphill battle to correct low-information communities on the internet. As I mentioned earlier, they could be doing nearly anything else with that time — resulting in a far more positive, productive, and engaging experience than getting shouted down by novices on the internet.

The term "knowledge subreddit" that I introduced is an oxymoron and a fallacy. These communities often have little to no educational or productive value. Realizing this is a key step in curating your information diet towards only high-quality sources, and freeing up more time for actual *doing* rather than simply discussing and scrolling.

Chapter 8
Reddit's Rude Redesign

Over several months in mid-2018, Reddit slowly began rolling out a redesigned version of its desktop site to users. It was the first time that the site's design had changed at all in an entire decade, and represented the first major overhaul of Reddit's appearance since its founding in 2005. I'll refer to the redesigned site as "new Reddit" and the original design as "old Reddit" because that's what Reddit refers to them as. Users can force these views of the site by navigating to old.reddit.com or new.reddit.com.

As the 2018 Reddit redesign rolled out, users were automatically opted in, although they could choose to modify their settings and permanently opt out in order to continue using the old interface. Users who were not logged in would see the new appearance by default, unless they specifically navigated to the old.reddit.com URL. Everybody was therefore forced to at least *try* the new design, if only for a couple of minutes until they found the setting to disable it.

The reaction (from those who bothered to comment on the redesign, at least) was overwhelmingly negative. We can absolutely point out some inherent bias in that those who have a poor experience are much more likely to provide feedback on a product or service than those who have a positive experience. Still, very few people had anything good to say about the new site design, and you can still find these threads from 2018 through internet search engines.

Some Redditors who had been using the site for a long time pointed out the irony that much of Reddit's current popularity and success could be attributed to a migration of users from the link aggregator site Digg. In 2010, users of Digg revolted against a controversial redesign of the site, flooding the front page with links to Reddit and declaring it "Quit Digg Day." This event single-handedly caused Reddit to permanently overtake Digg in web traffic over the following weeks, despite Reddit previously having a small fraction of Digg's traffic.

The 2018 Reddit redesign was criticized as being resource intensive and even lagging at times. But perhaps the most common complaint was that the new site fit drastically less information onto one page and required far more scrolling. On my twenty-seven-inch 1440p monitor with the browser set to one hundred percent zoom, I can see seventeen different submissions on the old Reddit design. A quick flick of the scroll wheel brings the remaining posts out of the twenty-five total on the page into view, and I can then choose to click to the next page for an additional twenty-five posts. On the new Reddit design, I can see somewhere between two and five posts at one time. The image posts take up more screen real estate, whereas the article links and text posts take up less. The most common situation browsing the /r/all feed is that I can see only two posts and a portion of the next one, because /r/all tends to be mostly image, GIF, and video submissions.

Let's estimate on the high end and take a user who is subscribed to communities that have fewer images and contain mostly text posts and article links; we'll say this user can see on average four posts at once on the new Reddit view.

That's still an absolutely breathtaking reduction in the information density on a single screen. At seventeen posts visible in the 1,440 pixels that make up my screen's height on old Reddit, I could see 425% more post titles before I needed to scroll than a user of the redesigned site on the same desktop computer. Additionally, the new Reddit site now scrolls infinitely, likely intended to keep users on the website for longer; on old Reddit I found that reaching the end of one of the pages of twenty-five posts was most commonly the point at which I would make the decision to close the browser tab rather than continuing to spend time on Reddit. Removing the "next page" button also removed the tiniest bit of mental friction that taking the action to click it represented, which was often enough to shatter that state of zombified scrolling that many of us have experienced.

The redesign has essentially stripped away users' autonomy when it comes to choosing which posts to view on the site. On the old Reddit view, one quickly skims the title of a post and maybe glances at the small thumbnail of an image. Only if a user finds the title and/or thumbnail sufficiently interesting do they then *decide* to expand the post to view the image or text submitted. On new Reddit, users do not get this choice. GIFs and videos automatically play as the user scrolls past them. Images are reduced in size a bit, but otherwise almost always fully visible (the exception being long, narrow images like comic strips which are cropped until a user clicks on them). The first dozen lines of text posts are visible as a preview. New Reddit was a marked change in that users would no longer parse the titles of posts and choose what to interact with. Rather, every post in your feed is now automatically allowed to interact with *you*.

This redesign wasn't a very user-friendly choice on Reddit's part, especially among their original user base of technology enthusiasts who seemed to most appreciate the efficiency offered by the minimalist, dense, text-based nature of old Reddit. But it *was* a decision very friendly to advertisers. On old Reddit, advertisements are interspersed with a similar appearance to other links: a text title with a button for the user to expand an image or video. There is a small megaphone icon to the left of the advertisement, and underneath the post is the text "promoted," both of which stand out in a unique light-blue font color that doesn't appear elsewhere on the site. There are two or three of these promoted posts per each page of twenty-five links on old Reddit. It's trivial for users to use that light-blue visual trigger to quickly recognize these posts as ads and simply subconsciously skip past them to the next post. In the over a decade I spent on Reddit, I can't recall a single time when I expanded one of these ads to view the image or video associated with it, let alone clicked on the included hyperlink.

By contrast, on the redesigned Reddit the first advertisement that I see is somewhere between the second and fifth posts in the feed, and every seventh or eighth post after that is another advertisement. The ratio of ads to genuine posts is about the same before and after the redesign. However, these ads now take up about half the height of my screen. If the ad is a video, it starts playing automatically like any other video post on new Reddit. The visual indicators that the post is an advertisement are additionally much more subtle than before; there is a small gray "promoted" text near the top of the post, which is stylized visually identically to the text present in that area on posts submitted by actual users.

One of the most common criticisms of the redesigned Reddit was that it made the site look like Facebook. This was likely entirely intentional for reasons which will become obvious in the next several paragraphs.

It's hard for anyone outside of Reddit, Incorporated to pin down accurate financial metrics on the site. Companies listed on United States stock market exchanges must submit quarterly financial reports to the Securities and Exchange Commission, which are made available as public information. Reddit is not a publicly traded company and is thus not required to release any data on their financials. Therefore, the only authoritative data on Reddit's ad revenue growth over time that we have are a few scattered data points over the years that the company has strategically chosen to release.

One early data point from 2014 was released because Reddit promised to donate ten percent of its ad revenue that year to charity. From this, we learn that Reddit made only $8.3 million in ad revenue in 2014.[17] In December 2020, Reddit's Chief Operating Officer Jen Wong disclosed to *The Wall Street Journal* that Reddit's ad revenue had totaled over $100 million for 2019, and was on track to rise over seventy percent for 2020.[1] In a 2021 bid for private equity funding, Reddit claimed that in the second quarter of 2021 alone they had achieved $100 million in advertising revenue.[18]

This is a sad sample size of just three data points. But we can make the basic conclusion that Reddit's rate of annual ad revenue growth has been consistently in the high double-digit percentages and has perhaps accelerated a bit in recent years if the Q2 2021 data point was not an outlier. How does this stack up compared to competing social media platforms, though?

In that late 2020 *WSJ* interview, COO Wong also disclosed for the first time Reddit's daily active user count: fifty-two million for October 2020. Wong's forecast for Reddit's 2020 advertising revenue increase was likely accurate, given that it occurred near the end of the year in December. An "over seventy percent increase" on "over $100 million in revenues in 2019" would likely put us somewhere in the realm of $170–220 million in ad revenue in 2020 depending on how fuzzy those estimates were. If we divide this estimate by the claimed fifty-two million daily active users, we can roughly estimate that in 2020 Reddit earned about $4 in Average Revenue Per

User (ARPU), however we can refine this calculation a bit.

The above is almost certainly an overestimate as we are dividing by a daily active user (DAU) count; typically technology platforms determine annual ARPU by dividing their quarterly revenue by their average monthly active user (MAU) count, then summing the ARPU from each of the four quarters in a year. However, we do not have a MAU figure direct from Reddit. MAU is always higher than DAU since every user does not return to the platform each day; Facebook for example in 2020 had a DAU/MAU ratio of about sixty-six percent[19], which indicates that of the total number of unique users on Facebook in a single month, about two-thirds of them were using the platform on a daily basis. If we assume that Reddit has a similar ratio of daily to monthly active users as Facebook, we can multiply the above estimate by that ratio, putting Reddit's Average Revenue Per User in 2020 closer to $2.67.

Based on Facebook's quarterly filings[20], I calculated that in 2020 Facebook's ARPU was $31.61. Using similar data released by Twitter[21], I calculated their 2020 ARPU at $20.26. Snapchat had $10.10 in revenue per user in 2020.[22] Reddit's value generated per user is among the lowest of any social media platform. Keep in mind, these figures are two years *after* they had redesigned Reddit. We have so few pre-2018 data points likely in part because the figures were so laughably abysmal that they were too embarrassing to release, despite Reddit having spent its entire existence to date attempting to achieve profitability (at the time of this writing, Reddit has never publicly claimed to have made an annual profit).

I postulate that the redesign of Reddit was done with the primary motivation of increasing advertisement revenue. Think about it as if you were an advertiser: would you not pay more to serve ads under the new Reddit design (where they claim more screen real estate and look more like genuine posts) compared to the old one? To that end, if Reddit's more profitable competitors all had similar systems for ad delivery — images and video ads scattered within a linear feed of posts submitted by genuine users — it simply made sense for Reddit to try to replicate that success by mimicking the delivery format of content and ads on their competitors' sites.

It likely goes beyond that, though. I believe that with the redesign, there was also a desire to attract a different type of user altogether to Reddit. To advertisers, all eyeballs are not valued equally. The more frequently and likely someone is to be influenced by advertisements in their decision to purchase a product or service, the higher that person's value to advertisers.

In a previous chapter, we examined how Reddit's initial user base mostly consisted of programmers, engineers, and those working in or studying other science and technology professions. It doesn't seem like a stretch to assume that this audience of younger, tech-savvy users likely employed ad blockers in far greater percentages than the average web user. Not only is a web host usually not getting paid by their advertisers when a user blocks ads, but they are paying for computing resources to serve content to that user, potentially creating a net loss.

As we can see by my analysis of Reddit's average revenue per user of about $2.67 in 2020, simply redesigning the site to mimic the content delivery mechanisms of its competitors did not bring Reddit's ARPU in line with those other social media sites. If this number is correct, it means that advertisers are willing to pay on average nearly eight times more to serve ads to Twitter users, and nearly twelve times more to serve ads to Facebook users compared to Reddit users. We can explain this with two main effects:

1. Users of Facebook and Twitter may be multiple times more likely to be persuaded by advertisements and convert to a sale than users of Reddit.
2. Reddit may have less actionable information regarding their individual users, and therefore are worse at targeting ads to specific desirable demographics. Advertisers are not willing to pay as much for these generic ads as they are to serve an ad to, say, a thirty-year-old male engineer in Massachusetts, information which social media sites like Facebook and Twitter can provide with far more confidence than a pseudonymous site like Reddit.

Even if a site switches to the most effective advertisement delivery system possible, users who competently and aggressively block ads from their devices will still generate zero revenue. A Deloitte survey conducted in 2017 declared the eighteen to thirty-four age group to be the most "adlergic," with over seventeen percent of them blocking ads across four or more types of traditional and digital media. Interestingly, the survey also found that in all countries studied, users who blocked ads most of the time were 200–400% more likely to be employed, have more education, and have higher incomes.[23] This demographic presents a tough but potentially lucrative nut to crack for advertisers. Young people make most of their purchases online, and those with more disposable income are obviously a coveted target of advertisers — but they are not allowing themselves to be reached. Of course, this is a longer-term problem for the advertisement industry itself to grapple with and adapt to.

An easy way for websites to defeat the ad blocking ability of most users, especially as more and more people are using smartphones as their primary internet access devices, is to convince users to consume content through their dedicated smartphone application (rather than the web browser where users have their ad blocker utility installed) as the vast majority of users do not employ tools like a Domain Name System sinkhole to defeat all advertisements on their device or home network. This is a big reason why pretty much every mobile site, including Reddit, is constantly pestering you to download their app, and certain offenders seem to be *intentionally* crippling their mobile websites in order to make their app more appealing. Furthermore, attracting users to a smartphone application offers numerous additional benefits such as the ability to send notifications to that user to lure them back into the app and increase their engagement with the platform. Phone applications also provide a treasure trove of personal data on users compared to what can be collected from a web browser, although to Reddit's credit I reviewed their privacy policy dated November 15, 2022, and it does not appear that their smartphone app currently harvests any additional data on users beyond what their website would otherwise collect.

Social media companies like Reddit that make most of their revenue by serving ads to their users have an additional trick up their sleeves to continue increasing their revenue per user if they are having trouble figuring out how to reach "adlergic" users. They can attempt to attract another demographic to their site, one which has proven to be a cash cow in that they tend not to block ads, and engage with those ads to convert to a sale more frequently. Convincing a Facebook user to start using Reddit could certainly be easier than convincing young, tech-savvy users to stop blocking ads. Expanding the site's demographic reach would be a complementary long-term strategy while concurrently figuring out how to effectively monetize the existing user base.

Further evidence that Reddit desired to attract new users

of a different demographic than their initial population is that the old Reddit was left intact and accessible to those who wanted to continue using it. This was likely a lesson learned from Digg's fatal misstep back in 2010. One has to imagine that if Reddit is at all a competent business, a calculation was performed between what would be gained monetarily from outright forcing old Reddit users to switch to the new site design, versus the risk of revolt leading to a "Quit Reddit Day." Reddit, Incorporated doesn't care if seasoned Redditors don't like the redesigned site, because the new look isn't meant to appeal to them. The new layout looks most like Facebook's interface in my opinion, but also has far more in common with other social media platforms like Instagram and Twitter than it does with the old version of Reddit, which would make it easier for users of these platforms to begin using Reddit.

Over four years post-redesign at the time of writing, no real efforts have been made to incentivize old Reddit users to convert to the new Reddit. This may indicate that the "old guard" is simply not a worthwhile demographic for the site to monetize. It's not uncommon to see desktop users of old Reddit claiming that they would quit the site entirely if forced to use the new design. In the meantime, these users continue to produce content on the old Reddit site which is consumed by users on new Reddit, demonstrating that they do have some value. As time goes on and new users continue to join Reddit, the percentage of users on new Reddit will likely continue to climb due to it being the default site experience. Whether old Reddit users will be allowed to exist on the site indefinitely remains to be seen, however it is clear to me that these users are probably an afterthought in Reddit's business strategy moving forward.

Economically, I believe that we are entering an environment where investors are growing tired of the supplications of thus-far-unprofitable technology companies claiming that they are going to scale their way into profitability using a near-infinite growth model. Cheerleaders of this methodology are finally being confronted with the reality that they never actually understood Amazon's business model, and that a company simply being in the tech sector and failing to turn a profit for a decade-plus while amassing market share might not be the only ingredients to replicate the success of Amazon. Once the speculative froth is blown away, the reality is that most of these tech companies should be assessed by similar fundamental valuation metrics and expectations as those applied to companies in other industries.

If this shift continues (as I suspect it will), tech companies posting double-digit increases in user growth or revenue growth will no longer be able to use that as a smoke screen to distract from commensurate increases in losses. They will need to show a convincing path towards climbing out of the pit as it were, by demonstrating actual progress in moving to a profitable business model on a per-user basis. Hand-waving this away by claiming that sheer scale will fix it at some nebulous point in the future seems it is becoming a less acceptable story.

Investor sentiment morphing in this regard is of course anathema to Reddit, Incorporated, which for eighteen years has failed to report a profit but would very much like to become a publicly traded company. Today, Reddit remains privately-held, with the majority of shares controlled by Advance Publications (the parent company of Condé Nast, which purchased Reddit back in 2006). The remaining minority of shares are held by various venture capital firms, holding companies, and personal investors, most of which are US-based. In a Series F private fundraising round led by Fidelity Management in August 2021, Reddit had a $10 billion post-money valuation.[24] In December 2021 Reddit submitted a confidential filing for an Initial Public Offering (IPO) with the

US Securities and Exchange Commission (SEC), which *Bloomberg* and *Reuters* said anonymous sources claimed was shooting for a valuation of over $15 billion.[25,26] Analysts initially expected Reddit's IPO to occur in the first half of 2022, but it's likely that general stock market turmoil and especially a souring technology sector have delayed those plans.

Just prior to the publishing of this book, new rumors emerged regarding Reddit's IPO. *The Information* reported in February 2023 that anonymous sources familiar with the matter claimed, "Reddit is far from profitability but has its sights set on finally going public later this year—likely in the second half." According to the article, Fidelity has valued Reddit at just $6.6 billion, less than half of the formerly-hoped-for $15 billion valuation when Reddit confidentially filed for an IPO with the SEC in December 2021.[27] This indicates that Fidelity had marked down Reddit's valuation even further relative to January 2023, when *Business Insider* reported that Fidelity's filings had valued Reddit at thirty-nine percent less than in late 2021.[28] Only time will tell if 2023 is finally the year that Reddit goes public. If and when they do, though, I suspect that their quarterly filings will confirm my earlier conclusion that Reddit's revenue per user is among the lowest of any social media platform.

Chapter 9
The Rise of Outrage Porn

I distinctly remember (as many of us do) the week in mid-March 2020 that was the onset of the coronavirus pandemic in the United States and the ensuing lockdowns. My employer had sent everyone home to work remotely, the threat level of the virus was not yet well-defined, and essentially every destination besides grocery stores shut down. With nowhere to go outside of home plus reclaiming the sum of time that I spent commuting and getting ready for work, the amount of free time that I had at my disposal skyrocketed overnight.

Like many people who did not have enough hobbies or the drive to fill that newly-acquired time productively, I was instead sucked into scrolling on the internet. Before this, my most recent attempt to quit Reddit in the late summer of 2019 did not last more than a few weeks, which I know because the blog that I started went dark in mid-September 2019 as I failed in my quest and once again began burning all of my free time on Reddit. The onset of the pandemic six months later elevated my Reddit usage to simply ludicrous levels.

In the latter majority of my tenure on Reddit, I did not often go to the /r/all or /r/popular feeds. I'd estimate it was around 2013 when "Advice Animals" memes were considered the peak brand of humor on Reddit that the front page had grown far too stale for me and I retreated into only browsing a curated list of my own communities. However, in those early pandemic days I was spending so many hours each day on the site that the subreddits I was subscribed to no longer produced enough content to occupy that elevated amount of time.

Desperate for additional content to fill my day (and partially curious to see evolving news on the virus) for the first time in many years I clicked over to the /r/all feed, which displayed the most popular posts across all communities on Reddit. I was expecting to find mostly news articles, some fun facts on science and technology, and lighthearted, barely-funny memes which had formed the core of Reddit's /r/all experience since I had joined the site in 2010. I found some of what I expected, but I was surprised to see Reddit's front page filled with something else: anger.

There were a half dozen or so subreddit communities that I had never heard of before that had posts sitting on the front page of Reddit. The common thread among all of them seemed to be rooted in getting angry at or mocking other people. I had seen anger on social media before, mostly on Facebook and in the context of people discussing politics. A curious development of these "new to me" anger-based Reddit communities was that many of the posts within them had no explicit link to politics.

The first one that I noticed was /r/MurderedByWords, which featured screenshots of social media interactions containing a "response which completely destroys the original argument in a way that leaves little to no room for reply." There was /r/PublicFreakout, "dedicated to people freaking out, melting down, losing their cool, or being weird in public." Perhaps needing the least explanation was /r/IAmATotalPieceOfShit, where users post social media screenshots or videos of others who they think fit the namesake for the community. Meanwhile, over in /r/IAmVerySmart, the users mock "people trying too hard to look smart."

In terms of firsthand experience, I can't possibly pinpoint when those communities began rising to prominence on Reddit, since I hadn't visited the /r/all feed for years prior. The juxtaposition from how I remembered the front page of Reddit was unmistakable, however, and my interest was piqued, so I began digging into this phenomenon. The perfect description for what I was observing was coined back in 2009, when journalist Tim Kreider created the term "outrage porn." In a *New York Times* article, Kreider wrote, "It sometimes seems as if most of the news consists of outrage porn, selected specifically to pander to our impulses to judge and punish and get us all riled up with righteous indignation."[29]

Outrage porn was precisely what these subreddits that I had never heard of before but were apparently now quite popular on Reddit were all about. The content in these communities was primarily various examples of people acting rudely, arrogantly, foolishly, irrationally, or immorally. If we ignore the political posts for now, in most cases the submissions to these communities showcase someone subjectively behaving poorly by societal standards.

A core concept of outrage porn is in taking those single examples of misbehavior and extrapolating them into character judgments. Such a broad, simplistic brush applied with their sample size of one incident allows viewers to confidently declare that the subject is generally just a bad person. Consequentially, if we as viewers feel anger towards the subject for not exhibiting acceptable in-group behaviors, that polarization leads to the conclusion that the subject must belong to the out-group.

Now add to the mix how readily and eagerly we humans desire confirmation bias, the tendency to search for, interpret, favor, and recall information in a way that confirms or supports one's prior beliefs or values. Continuing to follow this train of half-baked thoughts and logical fallacies, if for example "bad people" are the out-group, then it follows for the viewer that they must belong to the in-group of good people. If the out-group is defined by stupidity, the viewer concludes that they must be a smart person. Note Kreider's specific phrasing of "righteous indignation," identifying that this anger wells up from each of our individual perspectives where we see ourselves as model humans, veritable paragons of ideality.

One of the most creatively egregious videos that I saw baiting outrage from others was a seventeen-minute video of a woman purporting to show others how to paint a design onto their smartphone. The video features her creating a misaligned design with painter's tape on the back of the phone, "forgetting" to cover the camera lens before spray-painting over it, adding an obscene number of coats of spray paint to the phone, and pouring water over the phone at the end before finally peeling the tape off to reveal the uneven, runny, swamped mess of color she had turned the phone into. Throughout the video, she is incessantly narrating how amazing it looks. The video racked up millions of views, hundreds of shares, and thousands of comments on Facebook, with most of the commenters posting about how ugly the phone looked or how stupid the woman was for ruining it. They of course fell for it hook, line, and sinker, because those comments and shares are part of what Facebook uses to measure "engagement" which determines how many other users see the video show up in their feed. The woman's Facebook page was filled with these types of videos, such as another one featuring her creating a sticky disaster while demonstrating how to make cotton candy in a clothes dryer. She was laughing her way to the bank with these videos being monetized on Facebook. Many of her videos have made it to the /r/DiWHY subreddit (a play on words between the abbreviation for Do It Yourself and the word why, as in "why would anybody do this"), where just as on Facebook, Redditors swarmed to the comments to get their daily hit of illusory superiority by leaving a note disparaging the project or belittling her intelligence.

In my opinion, the main appeal of outrage porn is that it allows us to feel virtuous in exchange for zero investment of time or energy towards any effortful pursuit. You can watch a video of someone verbally abusing a service worker at a restaurant and think, "I wouldn't act that way." Next, you can scroll to a screenshot of a social media post from someone who looks like they put it through a thesaurus to find several rare words and think, "ha, what a pseudointellectual," concluding that since you found him out, you must be of superior intelligence. You can then scroll to a screenshot of someone replying with a witty one-liner straw man that purports to completely shut down the argument of an "outsider," for example a politician that you disagree with or whichever celebrity has been cast as a villain by a recent revelation. The sheer number of internet communities and platforms filled with content dedicated to outrage porn means that one can continue scrolling and reacting in this vein ad nauseam.

That's not to say that in *some* cases, the content presented in these communities isn't actually subjectively negative when judged by the standards of a civilized society. Even in those cases, though, there is zero value in us watching or reading it and forming judgments. Does keeping tabs on the negative ways in which some people whom you will never meet are acting affect your life in any appreciable way? Is being smarter than some of humanity's dumbest people something to hang your hat on? If you've simply surpassed the lowest possible bar of acceptable behavior, is that any reason to pat yourself on the back?

I suspect the cognitive dissonance at play here — with at least the subconscious realization of the above — is part of what makes outrage porn so addicting. One needs a constant "hit" as it were, because there is no real accomplishment from this activity, and deep down almost everybody knows that. There is no lasting sense of satisfaction as exists in volunteering one's time for a meaningful cause, building something useful with your hands, contributing some valuable item to the archives of human history, or simply living a virtuous life for its own sake.

Additionally, there's a darker side of outrage porn in that the subjects who "go viral" may not be the deserving victims that the jury of the internet paints them to be. Several of the posts in the /r/PublicFreakout community feature people who are clearly suffering from some degree of untreated mental illness. One user heavily mocked in the /r/IAmVerySmart subreddit for creating a post with verbiage that seemed sesquipedalian — overusing big words — was confirmed to be on the autism spectrum. In these cases, the users who engage with the content in these communities fail to distinguish themselves from middle school bullies.

One question at the forefront of my mind as I investigated this phenomenon was *when* these outrage porn communities had risen to prominence. As I mentioned earlier, I pretty much never went onto the /r/all and /r/popular feeds on Reddit during the latter half of the 2010s. But it's perhaps this absence that allowed me to realize that something had changed between the Reddit of 2013 and the Reddit of 2020. Our brains are much better at detecting large contrasts, whereas small changes over time can go unrecognized as we slowly adapt to the marginal differences.

So I took to using Reddit as a social archival tool, something which it is still remarkably good at. The earliest observation in the vein of noting outrage-based content *specifically* on Reddit that I can find was posted in May 2019 in the /r/UnpopularOpinion community, where a user's post begins, "Reddit is suffused with outrage porn." The user lists nearly a dozen communities and elaborates, "most of the content on these subs is simply pointing out how awful some random person is. Just how insanely, enragingly, blindingly awful they are. We spend a lot of time and energy just to be mad at someone we will never, ever meet or interact with." This user's post garnered nearly no engagement; just seventeen upvotes and two comments from other users.[30]

Several other text posts submitted by users expressed a similar sentiment, but that one from May 2019 is the earliest dated one that I could identify. Presumably this user had been exposed to this content for quite some time before getting fed up with it, so we likely need to go back a bit further to find the point when outrage porn began to become popular on Reddit.

Looking at the creation date of a specific subreddit community isn't a great indicator, as sometimes these communities are created and sit dormant for years before seeing much activity. Instead, we can look at the number of users subscribed to a particular subreddit over time and try to pinpoint a rapid increase in its growth rate of total subscribers. The website www.subredditstats.com shows a list of the top communities on Reddit sorted by number of subscribers. Additionally, it provides a handy graph of each community's historical subscriber count, along with several other related metrics.

From the top four hundred subreddits by subscriber counts, I selected a dozen which I think are a good representation of outrage porn content. Specifically, what I am looking for is an inflection point when the subscriber count of those communities began increasing at a much more rapid rate than what would be expected with the normal exponential growth of popular Reddit communities. This should also coincide with the community climbing the ranks of the most popular subreddits, indicating that it is gaining subscribers more quickly relative to other communities on the site. If this exists, it will help us pinpoint when users began engaging more heavily in outrage-based content on Reddit. Since this is publicly available historical data, anybody can go back and verify my claims.

One example to explain my methodology: the /r/IdiotsInCars subreddit had 94,880 users on December 31, 2017. By January 4, 2018, this community had surged to 107,241 users, an increase of thirteen percent in just four days. This was likely caused by a very popular post which got enough votes in the subreddit to rise into the /r/all and /r/popular feeds, encouraging users who did not know about the community but enjoyed the content to subscribe. Most importantly, following this event, /r/IdiotsInCars enjoyed a much higher subscriber growth rate than it had prior. For example, by the end of 2018, the community boasted nearly 650,000 subscribers, making it the 236th most-subscribed-to community on Reddit. It had started the year as the 1,064[th] most-subscribed-to, a remarkable gain relative to other subreddits.

I will follow the same methodology to identify this inflection point for my other selected outrage porn subreddits and summarize my findings in the following table.

Subreddit Name	Subscriber Inflection Point
/r/IdiotsInCars	January 2018
/r/PublicFreakout	August 2018
/r/Trashy	October 2016
/r/MurderedByWords	October 2017
/r/JusticeServed	Fairly steady growth since April 2015*
/r/IAmATotalPieceOfShit	June 2018
/r/IAmVerySmart	Fairly steady growth since October 2013
/r/QuitYourBullshit	April 2017
/r/AmITheAsshole	October 2018
/r/MaliciousCompliance	Fairly steady growth since May 2016
/r/InsanePeopleFacebook	November 2018
/r/EntitledParents	January 2019

*This community showed atypical activity in April 2015, going from zero subscribers to 5,000 over the course of only four days.

Interestingly, this analysis blew my initial speculation out of the water. My original hypothesis was that the rise of outrage porn on Reddit could be sourced to the site's 2018 redesign, because the new design had been successful in attracting users from other social media sites like Facebook and Twitter, and that those users had dragged the outrage in with them. That line of thought is clearly incorrect, as many of the inflection points in the growth of these communities occurred before the redesign began rolling out to users during the middle portion of 2018. A few had been enjoying steady exponential growth since several years before Reddit's redesign.

It's most likely then that outrage porn is simply a feature of the internet as a whole at this point that developed as a reflection of human tendencies, and was amplified by sorting and engagement algorithms on social media platforms. Research has indicated that popular or viral content on the internet was partially driven by high-arousal emotions in viewers. Content which evokes either highly positive emotions (e.g. joy) or highly negative emotions (e.g. anger, outrage, anxiety) was positively correlated to virality, even when researchers attempted to control for content which was surprising, interesting, or practically useful (all of which are also positively linked to virality).[31,32]

Additionally, the threshold for expressing outrage is likely lower online than in person.[33] On the web, one can safely express their condemnation of the wrongdoer by quickly typing out a highly-edited stream of their thoughts. Doing so in person, one's rebuke may not come out as suavely, and of course the dissenter's proximity to the person they perceive as a wrongdoer exposes them to the risk of physical violence if they initiate a confrontation.

A study of 1,252 adults across several days examined their exposure to both moral and immoral acts encountered in three areas: online, in person, and through traditional media (television, print, or radio). Interestingly, consistent for each setting, participants were over twice as likely to report learning about an immoral act than a moral act. Participants were more likely to be exposed to immoral acts online than in person or through traditional forms of media. Additionally, stronger feelings of outrage were evoked by participants when they learned about an immoral act online than through the other methods.[34] The implications are astounding — people are not only exposing themselves to more outrage-based content on the internet than they'd otherwise experience in their life, but they're getting angrier about it too!

Of course, social media companies know all of this as well; these multi-billion dollar enterprises most certainly have the resources to pay for consulting services from some of the top minds at the intersection of technology and behavioral psychology. And why wouldn't they, when your attention and engagement are at the core of their business strategy? But how far is too far, and when have these companies crossed the line in their quest to squeeze a few more dollars out of every user?

Speculation and criticism of Facebook in particular came to a head in October 2021, when thousands of internal Facebook documents were leaked by employee-turned-whistleblower Frances Haugen, who had worked on the company's "Civic Integrity" team but felt that her work to identify and fix the social network's problems was stymied. Seventeen media outlets coordinated with Haugen to release articles digging into the papers on October 25, 2021. Three days later, Facebook's Zuckerberg released an upbeat video announcing that the company was changing its name to Meta and focusing on a shift to virtual reality, which some critics claimed was an attempt to distract the public and lawmakers from the revelations unleashed by Haugen.

Of particular note in "The Facebook Papers" was the development path of the platform's system of user reactions. In February 2016, Facebook's "like" button was expanded to include five emoji reactions to posts: "love," "haha," "wow," "sad," and "angry." The leaked documents reveal that in late 2017, Facebook tweaked the algorithm that decides what users see in their news feeds to give emoji reactions five times the weight of a simple "like." The motivation was simple: posts that garnered an emotional reaction were proven to be more engaging, and it logically follows that more engaged users spent more time on the platform, thus making more money for the company.

Internal emails and memos from data scientists at Facebook warned of the negative effects of the changes to the algorithm — that it was amplifying anger on the platform more so than other emotions. "Misinformation, toxicity, and violent content are inordinately prevalent among reshares," noted the researchers. Company data scientists proposed changes to the algorithm such that it would not boost outrage and divisive content as frequently, however the documents show that Zuckerberg resisted many of the changes out of concerns that they would lower users' engagement with Facebook.

Discussing these algorithms naturally widens our discussion back to including all social media platforms, including Reddit. A central facet of debate over these algorithms and their effect on users and society at large is that they are black boxes. Legally, social media algorithms are protected as intellectual property; trade secrets which provide the company with a competitive advantage. Users have no right to inspect these algorithms, which will continue to be the case unless the laws change in a country large enough that social media companies would not want to be locked out of that market.

This algorithmic black box has shrouded Reddit now, too. Back in 2008, Reddit was still playing second fiddle to Digg with only about five percent of the latter's traffic. In an interesting twist which was certainly well-received by the technology community, Reddit decided to make nearly all of its code open-source (excluding only the portions that handled things such as spam detection to prevent these features being gamed). One cited motivation was that Reddit's team of just five employees at the time could be helped by users taking a look at the code and proposing various features and improvements. Reddit also boasted of a commitment to transparency, setting itself apart from other social aggregator sites like Digg which were frequently accused of having rigged algorithms. In a June 2008 interview with *CNET*, Huffman said, "One of our driving goals is to stay as open and transparent as possible and give our users an alternative to mainstream media...this is just the next logical step toward that goal of opening up the actual system." The article notes Huffman's surprise that Reddit's parent company Condé Nast quickly approved the decision to go open-source.[35]

Anybody with the technical know-how to decipher code could now peek under the hood by heading to Reddit's GitHub repository and learn exactly how Reddit functioned. Users could (and did) dig into Reddit's ranking algorithm. The algorithm that determined which posts were "hot" for example, was a simple little snippet of code. A logarithmic function was used to weight the first votes more heavily, that is, the first ten upvotes had the same weight as the next hundred. Downvotes were subtracted out to return a net score, and the time of submission was factored in to give preference to newer stories and ensure that old links would gradually fall off the page. Although voting bots have plagued Reddit for most of its existence, the open-source code with its relatively few variables meant that users could at least be assured of a *mostly* democratic process to content ranking and that Reddit was not manipulating secret variables behind the scenes like Digg, Facebook, and other social media platforms were suspected of doing.

The above was true up until September 2017. That is when Reddit made the announcement that their code would no longer be open-source; the GitHub repositories would be archived and left accessible but no new updates would be made. The main reason cited in the announcement was related to competition: "Open-source makes it hard for us to develop some features 'in the clear' (like our recent video launch) without leaking our plans too far in advance. As Reddit is now a larger player on the web, it is hard for us to be strategic in our planning when everyone can see what code we are committing." Users commenting on the announcement criticized the decision, correctly pointing out that open-source does not mean that all changes need to be available immediately, and that internal production code with new features could easily be kept private until those features were ready to be committed. Other commenters accused Reddit of "selling out" their users in favor of shareholders and investors.

In retrospect, this decision to go closed-source came at an interesting time — almost exactly seven months before Reddit began rolling out their new site design, which is probably not a coincidence. Has Reddit changed their post ranking algorithm in the years since they went closed-source? Could it be that Reddit is now playing with variables that boost content that fosters outrage and other emotional reactions in the name of increasing user engagement? Unfortunately, that information is now proprietary, and short of either a Reddit whistleblower or impactful legislation targeting social media companies' algorithms, we may never again know what is going on inside the black box of Reddit.

As the study of my dozen selected outrage-based communities on Reddit showed, several of these communities were on the rise before Reddit went closed-source, and before the redesign. That's proof enough that when Reddit was still under an open-source, democratic content ranking system, users were seeking out and subscribing to this content of their own volition. When there are algorithms at play on social media sites they may *amplify* outrage, anger, and other negative emotions, but the code is ultimately only feeding off the natural attraction that humans have shown towards engaging with this content.

It seems that these days we're more likely to find anger or outrage on the internet than anything else, whether we're browsing news sites or social media platforms. The algorithms can manipulate the flow of information that we receive, but ultimately they can't force a rational person to give up his or her autonomy. Recognizing that outrage porn has less than zero value to your life and choosing to completely opt out of it will drastically improve your internet experience, and potentially your offline life as well, by blocking out that constant stream of negativity. Ultimately, this may mean quitting these algorithm-driven social media sites entirely — Reddit, Facebook, Twitter, Instagram, TikTok, and whichever new ones will pop up after the publishing of this book. These sites are not the whimsical places to socialize, stay informed, and discover entertainment that we thought they were.

Chapter 10
Minority Rule

In the mid-2000s, a working hypothesis emerged among users of collaborative online spaces such as forums and wikis that became known as the 90–9–1 principle, which attempted to quantify the ratios of how strongly participants interacted with online communities. It claimed that only one percent of participants create content, such as forum threads and wiki articles. The next nine percent *contribute* to that content, by replying to or editing it, respectively. The remaining ninety percent of participants "lurk," meaning that they simply silently read and observe the content produced by the other users.

Several studies, both formal and informal, have purported to prove or disprove the 90–9–1 principle. Some have shown participation data nearly perfectly in line with the ratios, while others have found communities that show much higher rates of creators and contributors. In the end, regardless of the exact numbers, most have shown that the general rule of thumb bears out — participation in online communities is quite disparate, and a minority of highly active users produce the vast majority of content in these communities, which is then consumed silently by the lurking majority.

If this principle is true, what would this look like on Reddit? For one, Reddit has an additional degree of interaction compared to old-school forums, where users can post and reply to content but not vote on it. We could place users into groups based on how they interact with Reddit, then compare the groups based on their relative size to the total user base. I imagine that this hierarchy (descending in size from largest to smallest) would look like:

1. **Unregistered Lurkers**: These users do not have a Reddit account, and they mostly just read and observe the default /r/popular feed, perhaps manually navigating to a couple specific subreddits that have caught their interest.

2. **Registered Lurkers**: These users signed up for a Reddit account for the sole purpose of creating a customized feed of subscribed communities that they enjoy more than the /r/popular feed. They read and observe, but do not otherwise interact with the site.

3. **Voters**: Users who vote on posts created by other users (and the comments therein) as they navigate their front page feed on Reddit.

4. **Commenters**: This group interacts with their fellow Redditors by actively commenting in reply to submissions and comments created by other users.

5. **Submitters**: These users submit parent posts such as images, GIFs, videos, or text to various subreddit communities.

6. **Curators**: This group of users often sorts their feed by "newest first," making them some of the very first to vote on submissions to their subscribed communities.

A user is not mutually exclusively bound to one role in this list, and for that reason perhaps users could be allocated to these buckets in fractional proportion to how they invest their effort towards different activities on Reddit. Take an example user who only votes on every fifth post on average in their feed and spends only one percent of their time on Reddit writing comments. The fractional effort from this user could be distributed as 0.79 users towards Registered Lurkers, 0.20 users towards Voters, and 0.01 users towards Commenters.

This "Hierarchy of Reddit Interaction" follows the rule of thumb of the 90–9–1 principle: these groups that I have listed in ascending numerical order successively each have a fraction of the amount of user effort dedicated towards them as the preceding group. If graphed on a pie chart, the Unregistered Lurkers slice would be the majority of the chart, and the Curators slice would be the smallest, a tiny and barely-perceptible sliver.

Unfortunately, the data that I would need to *conclusively* prove out this hypothesis is proprietary. The above sorting of six buckets is based on a combination of extrapolation, speculation, and my own experience as a Reddit user for over a decade. With the small amounts of publicly available data from Reddit we can at least prove one of these hierarchical relationships though.

We can look at the number of posts and comments per day across several different subreddit communities to get an idea of the amount of effort that users have invested into these various activities. If my Hierarchy of Reddit Interaction holds any weight, then the number of comments should be vastly larger than the number of submitted posts. I am going to select some data points based solely off a random selection of subreddits of various sizes ranked by their number of total subscribers to try and get a fair sample. This data was sourced from www.subredditstats.com.

Subreddit Rank	Comments Past 24H	Posts Past 24H	Ratio of Posts to Comments
1	11011	232	0.021
51	1226	85	0.069
101	1009	130	0.129
251	1016	59	0.058
501	397	68	0.171
751	389	66	0.170
1001	66	14	0.212
1251	42	8	0.190
1501	881	75	0.085
1751	59	15	0.254
2001	35	6	0.171

At least between posts and comments, the hierarchy holds out — the randomly selected communities had anywhere from four times to fifty times as many comments as posts over the past twenty-four hours. The average across this sample with each community weighted equally was 0.139 posts per comment. While this says nothing about the number of *unique* users who are posting and commenting, the user-equivalent effort here when the totals are compared was remarkably close to the one-to-nine ratio (or 0.111) which would be suggested by the latter numbers in the 90–9–1 principle.

The main consequence of the 90–9–1 principle and my Hierarchy of Reddit Interaction is minority rule — a relatively small amount of user effort is being invested into performing the actions that decide the content that all users of the site will see. For example, each step down in the hierarchy, note that actions become progressively more impactful. Lurkers have zero impact. Users voting on content that is already on the front page have almost no impact. Commenters can shape what other users see when they read the comment section of posts, but their impact is ultimately limited by the fact that only a fraction of the users who see the post will venture into the comments.

Submitters of links, images, videos, and text posts to subreddit communities have an important role, as whichever subset of these posts becomes popular will make up the entirety of other users' feeds, and become the vector through which all other interaction occurs on Reddit. Curators who hang out in the queue of new posts have the largest impact of all. As we discussed in the prior chapter, when Reddit's code was open-source prior to September 2017, the voting algorithm used a logarithmic function. Assuming this is still the case, that means that the first ten votes on a post are equivalent in weight to the next hundred, which are themselves equivalent to the next thousand. The earliest users to vote on a post following its submission have the most power in regard to determining whether it will be shown to other users or not.

Logically, it follows that users who focus most of their time on Reddit into the latter two activities — submitting and curating — have several orders of magnitude higher impact in determining the content displayed on Reddit than users who rarely or never perform these activities. We would then apply a linear multiplier based on the amount of time the user spends on Reddit each day performing these actions, with users spending more hours on the site daily clearly having a larger impact.

Some Reddit users will say that the above conclusion does not matter to them. As long as they can log onto Reddit and be entertained, informed, outraged, and have their biases confirmed, they don't care where the content comes from. In my opinion, it raises an interesting counterpoint to the idea of Reddit as a democratic platform. Whether a post survives the "valley of death" of newly submitted posts and sees success is far more reliant on how well it appeals to the relatively few users who spend large amounts of time on Reddit curating the new submission queue.

Does it change your value perception of content on Reddit when a small percentage of users can have a vastly larger impact than the average user on what you see on the platform? What if you had full transparency as to who these curators were, and it was mostly a cabal of directionless losers who spend twelve or more hours per day on Reddit?

To some Redditors, this recognition did change things. In early 2020, an infographic began circulating on the site showing how six users had collective moderation privileges over 118 of the top five hundred subreddit communities. These users became known as "power mods," referring to their jurisdiction over a ridiculously large number of subreddits. Moderators on Reddit have the power to delete posts and comments at will, and even permanently ban users from their community for any reason, including just because they felt like it. According to Reddit's help documentation, moderators are "free to run their communities as they choose, as long as they don't break the rules outlined in Reddit's Content Policy or Moderator Code of Conduct."[36] The infographic was re-posted in several different communities over the next couple of months and many of these posts were removed, allegedly because publicly naming these power mods was leading to their harassment by Reddit users.

The most prolific power mods on Reddit have a hand in controlling hundreds of communities each. User "AwkwardTheTurtle" takes the crown as moderator of nearly eight hundred different subreddits, and many more accounts hold sway over triple digit counts of communities. It would seem to be an insurmountable challenge for a single person to effectively moderate more than a handful of forums, let alone an unpaid volunteer.

In the comments of these expository posts before most of them were removed, Redditors swapped anecdotes of their interactions with these power mods. Some users claimed to be victims of unfair bans and verbal abuse at the hands of the half-dozen users referenced in the infographic. Other Redditors speculated as to the power mods' motivations — proposals included that they were secretly employed by Reddit, that they sold their influence to third parties, or that they were simply motivated by a lust for authority. Someone leaked alleged screenshots from a Discord chat room where these power mods would gather to coordinate activities. Other users claimed (without hard evidence) that channels like that were also used for the power mods to exchange or trade moderatorships in different communities among themselves in order to consolidate their influence over Reddit. Whatever the truth of the exact details, the fact is that these power mods do exist and can exert control over a large swath of what tens of millions of people see on the front page of Reddit.

Additionally, over the past few years, many communities on Reddit have implemented automated tools to lighten the task load of moderation. AutoModerator (or AutoMod for short) is a Python script written by Reddit administrator "Deimorz" and is "a bot designed to automate various moderation tasks that require little or no human judgment." Initially designed for personal use in the communities that "Deimorz" was moderating, after a few years of testing and development AutoModerator was officially built into Reddit's tool suite in 2015. Any moderator can activate AutoMod in their subreddit, and can task the bot to automatically perform certain functions using the simple YAML scripting language.

For example, AutoMod can be set to automatically remove

any comment or post made by a user whose account is newer than a set threshold, or whose karma score is below a set threshold. These settings are an easy way to filter out spammers and other bad actors, who tend to accumulate negative karma quickly and create new accounts frequently after being banned. However, this approach also causes false positives in that legitimate new users to Reddit will be caught in these filters. The number of false positives will increase in line with the threshold values, for example, a community could require an account be two weeks old and have one hundred total karma before posting. Any competent bad actor will know this is occurring, probe the limits of the restrictions, and simply figure out the lowest effort way to get around them, while a genuine new user would not even know such capabilities existed on the site.

In many cases these filters are not even transparent to the user, for example the AutoModerator can remove posts and comments without sending any notification to the affected user. From the user's perspective their content will still appear to be present, however users other than moderators cannot see or interact with it. An incredibly small number of communities notify the user that their content was removed, but the vast majority of communities engaging in this practice do not. Due to the clandestine nature, in internet parlance this is referred to as "shadow" or "stealth" removal. A Redditor can check whether their content is affected by logging out, or simply opening a private browsing window and checking if their comment is present under the URL of the parent submission that they replied to.

Obviously, as the number of subreddit communities filtering content in this manner increases, earning the ability to participate on the site becomes paradoxical. In recent years there have been many posts submitted by new users to the /r/help subreddit complaining that they can't post in communities because they don't have karma, and they can't gain karma because they can't post anywhere. The usual response is for these users to gain karma by participating in subreddits without restrictions, but this is a poor solution as an increasing number of subreddits continue to implement such AutoModerator rules. In many cases it isn't transparent to the user which communities have these restrictions and which do not; in fact, the vast majority of users likely aren't even aware that their content is being automatically and silently filtered at all.

The original intent of automatically removing comments using stealth moderation tools was not censorship, but simply to hold those comments for manual vetting by a human. However, it appears that in most large subreddit communities this grew to be too intensive of a task for moderators to keep up with. To test this, I made a brand-new Reddit account and I left a comment on five random posts that were on the front page of Reddit. The comments were concise, fairly innocuous and on-topic. As expected, my comments appeared to be posted from my perspective, however when I opened the link in a private browsing window it was clear that each of them had been removed. I checked back into that account a week later and sure enough, no moderator in any of the five subreddits I had commented on had ever come around to approve any of those comments. At that time I tried commenting in the same communities, and two of them allowed my content through as I had clearly passed some arbitrary account age threshold.

This is an incredibly user-unfriendly approach to moderation. AutoModerator shadow removals are in most cases not transparent. A new user invests effort into creating content on the expectation that others will see it and interact with it, but instead their submission is instantly sent into a digital void by a bot, likely never to be seen again. Additionally, censorship of certain topics is made incredibly easy through automation, since any post or comment containing specified keywords can also be shadow removed. AutoModerator presents the ripe opportunity for abuse under Reddit's current system, where moderators are allowed to make whatever decisions they wish regarding policing content in the communities they control. These unpaid volunteers are for the most part unaccountable unless they commit egregious violations of Reddit's policies resulting in widespread, sustained outcry.

As usage of these automated tools continues to rise, it begs the question of how effectively they can be used to identify bad actors. Knowing the flaws of Reddit's karma system and the manner in which users tend to downvote content that they disagree with regardless of factuality, are negative karma scores a sufficient barometer to label a user as a troll? At the time of this writing, AutoModerator can only filter content based on the user's *total* post or comment karma, and users who participate in good faith across several communities nearly always have positive total karma scores. Having a negative total score across all of one's comment submissions over a fair sample size of communities on the site is generally a good sign that a user is incredibly rude or a troll.

However, a popular requested feature by moderators is to allow AutoModerator filtering based on karma in a specific subreddit community. This would be an incredibly dangerous feature that could amplify the echo chamber effect of Reddit if it were to be implemented. For example, imagine a community that sets a rule that any user with community karma less than zero automatically has all of their content removed. This would mean that any new user who got a negative reception on their very first comment in the community would effectively have that account permanently shadowbanned from participating there ever again. Such a rule would elevate the Reddit hive mind's ability to hide speech they disagree with using downvotes into silencing these users completely, effectively deputizing the community's groupthink with moderation abilities. Individual Redditors don't collectively deserve that power, when moderators have more than enough as it is.

Any moderator of a large subreddit community has the ability to significantly shape the content that tens of millions of users see (or perhaps more importantly, *don't* see) across a significant portion of Reddit. A regular user obsessed with curating content on Reddit only has a single downvote with which to attack content, whereas moderators can instantly remove anything — or anybody — they desire with impunity, even when that user has not violated broader Reddit policies. In an era of unprecedented digital media consolidation and rising amounts of misinformation, are you truly okay with your content being curated via minority rule by a small group of terminally online users?

Chapter 11
Astroturfed

When discussing Reddit's redesign, I mentioned that a commonality between the old and new site designs was how "sponsored" or "promoted" posts (i.e. advertisements) are interspersed with similar appearances to posts by genuine users on the site. This has been the case since Reddit opened itself to advertisement in 2009. Advertisers could enter a title and URL for their ad, put in a bid (determining how much time they get on the home page relative to what others paid), and optionally disable comments on their ads.

That last bit proved to be a fatal and quite humorous flaw in Reddit's advertising system. You see, comments were enabled by default, and users took full advantage. The comments would range from silly jokes, to airing grievances with the company and its products, to pointing out any lies or exaggerations in the ad. If the techie user base that had settled on Reddit could unite on just one issue, it was a distaste for advertisers invading their digital spaces.

Despite this pushback from Redditors, I recall the majority of ads having comments enabled for several years after I joined Reddit in 2010. It was almost like companies were viewing it as a challenge to find an advertising strategy that received positive reception among Reddit users. Today, it is exceedingly rare to find a "promoted" post on Reddit that has comments enabled — the default setting now is for that feature to be disabled, though I can't pinpoint an exact date when this was changed.

This guerrilla resistance waged in the comment sections of ads doesn't appear to be common knowledge among users today. Several articles and threads discussing the history of advertising on Reddit (which I read while researching the topic for this book) glossed over this bit of trivia. However, it's incredibly important because this reaction by users was physical proof of what became common knowledge among digital advertisers: Redditors hate ads.

Take the title of this 2014 article from *Ad Age*: "Reddit Hates Marketing. How to Market on It Anyway."[37] Clearly, advertisers were not scared off by their unwelcome reception and instead chose to adopt alternative tactics. What a nut to crack: if you could advertise successfully on Reddit, you could probably do so anywhere on the web. Many articles, videos, and even paid courses have been released over the years that claim to reveal all the secrets to running a successful advertising campaign on Reddit.

The answer may have evaded corporate marketing suits but was obvious to anybody who spent a fair amount of time on Reddit observing and interacting with actual users; above all else, Redditors hated *self*-promotion. Companies paying to promote their own content or users submitting links to their own website seem especially disingenuous when inserted into a feed of real people sharing links and images from around the web which they found informative, interesting, or entertaining. The solution to a much more successful and lucrative advertising campaign on Reddit was astroturfing.

Taking inspiration from the synthetic grass brand of the same name, astroturfing is essentially a fake grassroots movement. The term was coined in 1985 by Texas senator Lloyd Bentsen, originally in reference to politics. Astroturfing is a deceptive practice intended to create the impression of a grassroots origin (i.e. from common or ordinary people) in support of or in opposition to something, when in reality no such support exists. Applied to advertising, an example of astroturfing would be if a representative from a company posted a positive review of their product on Reddit, posing as a genuine end user who just happened to be satisfied with the product. There are several degrees of this type of advertising, ranging from simple product placement in an unrelated image or video, to gushing testimonials.

When overlaid with advertising industry data, the motivations for advertisers to engage in astroturfing are obvious. According to a 2022 survey by *BrightLocal*, forty-nine percent of customers trust online consumer reviews just as much as personal recommendations from friends and family, and a further twenty-eight percent of people trust online consumer reviews as much as professionally-written articles by topic experts.[38] *Adweek* found that seventy-six percent of consumers are more likely to trust content shared by "normal" people over content shared by brands.[39] In essence what this means is that the majority of people place a high value on testimonials from strangers online, and would be much more likely to purchase a product when it seems to be reviewed by a genuine customer as opposed to a blatant ad.

The primary goal of astroturfing in the context of online advertising is for the advertiser to appear to be an ordinary customer. Therefore, in the absence of incompetence on the part of the advertiser, they can be hard to discern from a user who is simply offering a helpful recommendation or is passionate about a product or service.

It's pertinent to note that in many countries, astroturfing at least in the context of marketing and advertising is illegal. In the United States, the Federal Trade Commission is able to levy fines upon those who violate its "Guides Concerning the Use of Endorsements and Testimonials in Advertising". However, in order to be fined, one first needs to be caught, and also be worth the time and effort to prosecute. Small, owner-operated businesses especially may either accept this tiny risk, or not even know that they are crossing legal lines while engaging in what they view simply as aggressive social media marketing.

In the grand scheme of online misinformation, marketing and advertising are relatively innocuous compared to many of the activities taking place on sites like Reddit. Astroturfing gets far more insidious than deceptively trying to sell a product. It can and is being used to boost various political and social agendas.

For example, one subreddit based on reposting tweets from prominent American left-wing politician Alexandria Ocasio-Cortez, /r/MurderedByAOC, regularly saw posts surge into the /r/popular and /r/all feeds on Reddit during 2021, despite only ranking around two-thousandth in the list of subreddits by number of subscribers. Communities that small simply never get to /r/all or /r/popular consistently, which one can verify by checking subreddits of a similar size and acknowledging that they have never heard of them. Every single submission to /r/MurderedByAOC was from one user, who was also the only moderator of the community (and additionally the creator and head moderator of several other political communities on Reddit). Many of the comments from users were copied and pasted verbatim from past comments in the community, drawing suspicion from other Redditors that they were bots controlled by this moderator.

Nearly every aspect of the above subreddit seemed manipulated and non-organic to users with critical thinking skills. The sole moderator was finally suspended by the Reddit administrators in June 2022, with no public reason given for the move. Yet Redditors had been raising questions and gathering their own evidence for at least two years prior that showed a convincing argument for flagrant violations of Reddit's Terms of Service by this account. Indisputable proof existed that in other communities that this account moderated, they were removing the existing top posts submitted by other users upon creating their own submissions in order to rocket them to the front page, a practice which the Reddit administrators stated "amounts to vote manipulation and thus is not something we can allow or support" back in 2017.[40]

Why was this moderator able to engage in a practice against Reddit's Terms of Service for so long before action was taken? The ability to illegitimately boost posts to the front page of one of the top ten most visited websites in the United States for two-plus years is quite the influential power. How many other accounts out there were performing their own astroturfing, but were not so horridly blatant about it that they could be caught by dozens of regular Reddit users?

For candidness, let's take a look at astroturfing on the other side of the American political spectrum on Reddit. I am quite certain that my readers outside the US — perhaps inside as well — are likely tired of hearing about our politics, however the dominance of American political discourse on Reddit makes it a tempting target for astroturfing, and thus provides prominent examples that are familiar to many Reddit users with which to prove my point.

During the 2016 US presidential election, the subreddit /r/The_Donald was created in support of then-candidate Donald Trump. Users browsing the /r/all feed on Reddit noticed something peculiar during the spring of 2016; multiple posts from /r/The_Donald were making it into that feed daily, at a much higher frequency than Reddit communities with many times more subscribers. The trick, it turns out, was that moderators in that community were applying a "sticky" to keep any new posts that they wanted to amplify at the number one post slot in the community. This would act as a "Bat-Signal" for other users (and potentially bots) to upvote the post. Stickied posts were not eligible for inclusion into /r/all, however when the moderators un-stickied the relatively young post with high engagement, it would rocket onto the front page of Reddit.

Site administrators considered this an exploit and struck back with a change to the /r/all algorithm in mid-June of 2016. The stated purpose was "to prevent any one community from dominating the listing. The algorithm change is fairly simple—as a community is represented more and more often in the listing, the hotness of its posts will be increasingly lessened. This results in more variety in /r/all." A few days earlier, an announcement by Reddit administrators hinting at the upcoming change said that it would "prevent vote manipulation."

The latter statement is hilariously ironic given that five years later, blatant evidence of manipulation of Reddit's front page by community moderators was still occurring, as noted in our first example. Reddit had a history of experience with this near-exact scenario — even down to the topic of the guilty communities both being US politics — but still the moderator of /r/MurderedByAOC was able to manipulate content onto /r/all in 2021. Notably, this went on for much longer than /r/The_Donald was able to get away with. Was Reddit willing to look the other way for as long as they could when the manipulation aligned favorably with the beliefs of those who control Reddit? Co-founders Huffman and Ohanian have certainly demonstrated that they are left-leaning in my opinion, and the Newhouse family who own Advance Publications (and thus Reddit) were noted as Democrataffiliated by *Forbes*[41], a claim which their company's political monetary contribution history as published by *OpenSecrets* corroborates.[42]

The ensuing deterioration in the relationship of /r/The_Donald users with Reddit would lead to perhaps the greatest public incident of abuse of power in Reddit's history. In November 2016, Reddit banned the /r/PizzaGate subreddit which was dedicated to discussing a conspiracy theory related to left-wing politicians and a clandestine pedophile ring, giving the reasoning that the community was exposing peoples' personal information. In response, users of /r/The_Donald began hurling expletives and abuse at Reddit co-founder and CEO Steve Huffman over the course of several weeks, tagging his user account "spez" in comments such that his Reddit inbox would be filled with constant notifications containing insults. A couple of days later, /r/The_Donald users began noticing that their comments had been retroactively changed without their consent. Instead of insulting Huffman, the comments had been silently altered to replace his Reddit username with those of the /r/The_Donald moderators, making it look like the user was insulting them instead. When a Redditor edits their own post or comment it acquires an asterisk next to it to indicate that it has been changed, and hovering over the asterisk displays the time when it was edited. But that indicator was not present in these cases, and several users brought forward hard evidence with before-and-after screenshots showing their comments had been silently changed.

Having been cornered, Huffman submitted a post to /r/The_Donald confessing to editing the users' comments via his "spez" account with administrative privileges, concluding, "As the CEO, I shouldn't play such games, and it's all fixed now. Our community team is pretty pissed at me, so I most assuredly won't do this again." *The Washington Post* interviewed Huffman following the incident, and reported that he claimed he was going to edit the names for just a few hours to give the subreddit's moderators a taste of what he had been experiencing for days, then intended to switch the posts back. The article also indicates that Huffman was perfectly aware what he did was a violation of Reddit's employee policies.[43]

The fallout on Reddit and in the technology media was massive. The crux of the issue doesn't hinge on whether one feels that the users of /r/The_Donald who had their comments edited deserved it or not, whether it was funny, or whether the outcome led to no tangible harm to anybody aside from bruised egos. Many Redditors left comments saying that despite their personal dislike for Trump and his supporters, they felt that Huffman crossed a line and permanently violated their trust in Reddit. Several users called for his resignation. The true shock to users was that Reddit administrators (i.e. employees) had the ability to stealthily edit users' posts with no indication that the post had been modified, which nobody outside of Reddit, Incorporated was previously aware was possible. This revelation was of course magnified by the context of this event — that Huffman in his multirole capacity as co-founder, CEO, and an administrator of Reddit would flippantly use this power in a knee-jerk emotional reaction to some childish trolling, and that in his ensuing apology would so nonchalantly reveal to the world that he (and likely other Reddit employees) could silently edit the posts of anyone on Reddit.

A week later, Huffman offered a more lengthy apology on Reddit, writing in part, "While many users across the site found what I did funny or appreciated that I was standing up to the bullies (I received plenty of support from users of [/r/The_Donald]), many others did not. I understand what I did has greater implications than my relationship with one community, and it is fair to raise the question of whether this erodes trust in Reddit." He also offered a couple of new features on Reddit. The first was that posts from /r/The_Donald (and only that one community) would no longer be able to appear in /r/all if they had been stickied at some point. The second was adding a long-requested feature to enable users to filter specific subreddits that they did not wish to see out of the /r/all feed. A user commenting on an *Ars Technica* article reporting this development said, "My main issue with his response is that it sounded like 'I'm really sorry for what I did, now here's the restrictions we're putting in place to suppress [/r/The_Donald].'"[44]

Notably, a feature to indicate when a user's post had been edited by a Reddit administrator was not among the olive branches offered by Huffman. Nor was it addressed *why* such a power existed in the first place — if a post or comment breaks the law or Reddit policies, there is no circumstance where removing said post entirely would not be equally or more effective than editing the content of it. The insinuations generated by this event caused some users to question the integrity of anything they had read in the past, or might read in the future on Reddit. Was this the first occasion that users' posts had been edited by site administrators, or simply the first time anybody had noticed? Were Redditors apparently just supposed to take Reddit's word and trust that they will self-monitor site administrators not abusing this stealth editing feature in the future? Unfortunately, this incident with Huffman was just another entry in an incredibly long tale of manipulation on Reddit.

Aside from moderator and administrator manipulation (which are obviously not powers available to everyone), there are practices that any Reddit user can engage in to make their astroturfing more effective. A query for "buy Reddit upvotes" on your internet search engine of choice will return many providers of such services. Selling or buying voting influence on the site is against Reddit's Terms of Service and can result in a ban from the site, however given site administrators' prior ineptitude with tackling manipulation and misinformation on Reddit, it may be prudent to call into question their ability to clamp down on vote buyers and purveyors. A December 2016 video published by journalism startup *Point* titled "Reddit For Sale: How We Bought The Top Spot For $200" details how the investigators submitted what was essentially an advertisement to Reddit's massive /r/videos community, bought thousands of upvotes from a third-party service, and watched their submission become the hottest post in that community.[45]

Some astroturfers go so far as acquiring multiple Reddit accounts in order to create a flurry of false consensus appearing to come from different people, seeding the desired illusion of more widespread support for their content. In internet terminology, these alternate accounts controlled by a single user are known as "sock puppets." Sometimes these actors create and curate their sock puppets themselves, but Reddit accounts can also be purchased on numerous sites around the web (again, a practice which violates Reddit's Terms of Service). Ideal sock puppet accounts are referred to as being "seasoned," meaning that they have an established post and comment history on the site which appears to be from a genuine user. This makes the sock puppet's content appear far more authentic compared to a brand-new account which has no previous activity beyond supporting one product or viewpoint. Older Reddit accounts with a consistent activity history and high karma scores sell for commensurately more money, representative of their potential value in being repurposed to boost other content.

Reddit is consistently ranked in the top ten most visited sites in the United States, and the top twenty worldwide. The tens of millions of eyeballs that traverse the site daily makes the motivations for astroturfing obvious. Whether someone or some group is trying to sell a product or promote a particular agenda, you can bet that many of them would exploit any possibility to get a leg up to gain more access to an audience of that size.

Avoiding the largest communities on Reddit as well as the /r/all and /r/popular feeds allows one to opt out of most of the social engineering attempts, such as political astroturfing. The advertising astroturfers, however, are rife at all levels of the site. Some are looking for that moonshot exposure on /r/all or a massive subreddit. Others trawl smaller hobbyist communities, looking to consistently promote and shill their products and content to a targeted niche audience.

At best, these actors are an annoyance; at worst, they are shadowy manipulators of peoples' emotions and thoughts. Clearly, Reddit has failed in the past at quickly identifying and taking action against astroturfers, as we saw in the example of the blatantly abusive manipulation by the political subreddit moderator that went on for years. There's an implication, perhaps borne of wishful thinking or naïveté, that the most popular content that we see on sites like Reddit has been democratically curated by our fellow users; this is shattered by the frequency with which proven inorganic activity has plagued Reddit's long history.

One could reasonably make the argument from an individualist perspective that it is the responsibility of each individual web user to be a critical viewer, taking a skeptical approach to every single thing they read on platforms like Reddit. There is indeed merit to that viewpoint, and we should absolutely recognize the slippery slope in calling for these platforms (or the government) to be the arbiters and enforcers of defining misinformation. I think most people would be in agreement that if these social media platforms are going to turn themselves into algorithmic black boxes, making it harder for individual users to suss out unfair abuse by bad actors, should not the responsibility to swiftly and effectively deal with such manipulators fall to the platform? What would Reddit's /r/all feed look like if every user was truly participating on a level playing field?

Let's switch gears to a tangential topic to astroturfing that I feel needs to be discussed, which is the issue of fake content. That is, content submitted by an online user which purports to record or retell some event as authentic, but is in actuality a complete fabrication. In recent years, the discussion of online misinformation and its impacts has continued to brew. Most commonly when people think of misinformation today, political news is probably the preeminent subject that they make an association with. However, it goes beyond the news and pervades all levels of our digital spaces. People are also amusing themselves with fake entertainment.

It sounds like such a silly thing to make a fuss about. For millennia, we humans have been entertaining ourselves with fiction. Plays, books, television shows, movies, and music which are based on exaggerated or completely fabricated events comprise a large portion of our species' cultural catalog. These fantastical tales can capture our imaginations through masterful artisanship, and occasionally present tangible lessons that we can take back with us to the real world. We all know the deal, though — we are transported to these pretend worlds for a temporary stay, with the full acknowledgement that such events did not truly happen.

Contrast the above with fake entertainment in the age of social media. The purpose of these platforms is to look into the lives and thoughts of other people, sometimes friends and sometimes strangers. The implication is that content created by the users of these platforms about their lives is an authentic experience, and that their post accurately portrays an event that happened to them. This assumption has of course been taken advantage of for nearly as long as social media has existed in order for people to project a carefully crafted ideal of what they want others to think their life is like. Reddit is no exception in falling victim to this phenomenon.

A common type of fake entertainment on Reddit comes in the form of videos. In this case, the implied context of many of these videos is that it's a spontaneous event that occurred somewhere out in the world. Sometimes the context will be someone intending to record an innocuous event where something "unexpected" then happens, such as an interaction between family members with a funny or shocking twist. Other times we'll get the impression that an event in public was fortuitously captured by a quick-thinking bystander who swiftly pulled out their smartphone to capture it, such as a prank being played on somebody or a dramatic argument.

Quite frequently these videos are reposted to sites like Reddit from other social media platforms where they originated, such as TikTok, Instagram, or YouTube. The most interesting aspect to me is that some of these videos are incredibly obviously staged, yet make it to the front page of Reddit anyway. If you have to ask, "why did they happen to be filming a video prior to this," it's probably staged. If the video portrays someone suavely accomplishing a difficult and lucky task in one go, it was likely recorded dozens of times to get the perfect cut. If the video features dialog that would fit seamlessly into a sitcom, it's probably scripted.

Puzzlingly, when I would head to the Reddit comment section of these videos expecting to find dozens of users pointing out that it was fake, I would find almost nobody doing so. Occasionally for fun I would expand all the Reddit comments and use the find command on my browser to look for keywords such as "fake," "staged," or "scripted." The most common scenario I found was that among the thousands of comments a video on /r/all generates, just a small handful of users with passed-over comments were remarking that they thought the video was not authentic.

I recall one commenter in particular who, in response to another user calling out a reposted TikTok video as staged, said something along the lines of, "I don't care if it's real, it could have happened to somebody." I find that to be a paradoxical perspective, because as I mentioned earlier, the entire implication of social media is that we're peering into other peoples' lived experiences. Fiction deceptively presented as reality abuses this assumption, and should therefore invalidate some of the entertainment value that we derive from this content.

Another popular form of fake entertainment on Reddit is in the form of stories. Several very popular communities on Reddit have disabled submission of links and images, such that only text posts submitted by users are allowed. In these communities, users often present a retelling of events that supposedly occurred in their life for reactions, advice, or simply for the entertainment of others. In /r/AmITheAsshole, users describe a situation they were involved in which elicited negative reactions from others, while community members debate and vote about whether the original poster was in the right or not. Next, you can head over to /r/MaliciousCompliance where users post stories about how they strictly complied with a rule in technicality, inflicting harm completely by the book on another party who is usually presented as a deserving villain. The subreddit /r/PettyRevenge follows a similar theme, where users post "stories of small victories over those who've wronged you." /r/Confessions is a place where users do just as the title implies, and positions itself as a place for people to share things that they need to get off their chest. The list of these story-centric communities goes on and on.

It doesn't take much skepticism to see that a decent amount of these stories are wildly unrealistic, generously one-sided on behalf of the poster, or otherwise give themselves away by the dialog presented simply not representing how actual humans interact with each other in the real world. A *Vice* article written by Amelia Tait in 2020 titled, "Some of Reddit's Wildest Relationship Stories Are Lies. I'd Know – I Wrote Them," interviews several people who write fake stories on Reddit. Apparently, their motivations for doing so are "a way to hone their creative writing skills while also making people laugh."[46]

Not infrequently, Redditors submit a post to Reddit itself fessing up to having a penchant for creating fake stories on the site. Some users report the same desire to just practice their creative writing. Others admit they like the karma points they earn for their submission, or basking in the flood of attention from other users if one of the posts becomes popular. A few users cite more devious motivations rooted in trolling, and confess that they primarily enjoy the aspect of tricking others.

Interestingly, it seems the moderators of /r/MaliciousCompliance became tired of users pointing out inconsistencies and discussing whether stories were fake, because "it's much more fun if we give people the benefit of the doubt." Redditors are notified by a subreddit rule which reads, "Don't discuss the validity at all. Don't claim it's untrue. Just don't." Those who violate this rule are apparently subject to a permanent ban from the subreddit without warning. Users in the /r/HumansBeingBros community are likewise informed that they will face a temporary or permanent ban from the community for posting comments such as "this is fake," asking why an event was filmed, or commenting that they believe that a submission was staged for upvotes or clout. The rule continues, "Pot-stirring, trolling or bad-faith commentary about our content or its authenticity will not be allowed. Discussion about the provenance and authenticity of submissions will be removed. Evidence must be provided if you suspect a specific post is staged."

Those rules all seem rather extreme, unless one's goal is to create an audience consisting almost completely of the most gullible users on the internet. How many users were commenting that they doubted the authenticity of submissions that these moderators felt the need to start banning them to prevent upsetting the illusion? This furthers my earlier assertion that fiction presented as reality on social media simply isn't that entertaining. If being told that something is probably fake ruins your enjoyment of it, it likely wasn't that well-written or constructed to begin with. Fans of science fiction and fantasy books, movies, games, and television shows obviously know that the events depicted are fake yet enjoy them anyway. Anyone pointing out why the events depicted could never have actually occurred would likely be met with speechless dumbfoundedness at their ability to state the utter obvious. Consumers of fake online content, however, often react with derision and hostility when a case for it being staged or scripted is presented, likely a psychological defense mechanism against the assertion that their cognitive faculties were insufficient to prevent them from being fooled.

On the other hand, we could go to the opposite extreme and simply assume that every story on Reddit is fake — each and every one a creative writing exercise of varying quality. This would certainly be a pragmatic and conservative approach to the fact that we cannot say with complete certainty which stories are fabricated and which are true. If you're going to entertain yourself with fantasy, though, you may as well dive into the boundless seas of higher quality, more enjoyable sources of it than short stories and videos found on Reddit or elsewhere on the web.

Personally, my frustration with this fake entertainment was a motivating factor for quitting Reddit and other social media sites, as well as refusing to engage with emerging platforms that seem susceptible to being infected by it. These communities are self-selecting for groups of people who are dumb enough to eat up the fake content and beg for more. You can avoid most fake content by staying off /r/all and /r/popular and not browsing the subreddits that are the primary offenders of pushing these fake stories and videos, but the frequency with which this fake content gets to the front page of Reddit certainly indicates *something* about the critical thinking skills of the people who browse these feeds. At times, I wished I could shout from the rooftops of Reddit, "This is all a lie, constructed to do exactly what you are all doing here: voting on it, talking about it, and potentially sharing it somewhere else!" But that would be a waste of time. Perhaps they're happy in their saccharine bubble. Anyone who sees the fraud for what it is, likely also recognizes that Reddit is rotten to the core and that one is better served by simply leaving than by wasting their time and effort trying to fight against it.

Chapter 12
Are Your Thoughts Your Own?

Humans are no doubt social creatures, and the desire to share and receive thoughts and ideas — then especially building upon the best contributions of others — has been a mainspring of the intellectual and cultural achievements of our species. Lately though, I have been questioning whether we humans are built to deal with an endless deluge of thoughts and opinions from hundreds (or thousands) of acquaintances and complete strangers on a daily basis. Surely no medium of exchange prior to social media allowed us to attain such deep access to the streams of consciousness of so many average people.

Today, ubiquitous smartphone access has democratized access to the internet. Those who are old enough to remember the unveiling of the iPhone may recall some of the general buzz at the time about how this was a *computer* in our pockets! The encyclopedic knowledge of humanity would be at our fingertips anywhere, no longer tethered to libraries or our clunky desktop and laptop computers! The promise of the iPhone was as a multi-tool: maps, music, a phone, and an internet browser, all in one intuitive device! The level of near-constant connectedness that these devices would usher in was unforeseen.

Let us for a moment think back to the methods of exchanging thoughts and ideas prior to the internet. For the entirety of human history, most people accomplished this primarily through face-to-face interaction. This has the very obvious limitation of restricting us to interaction with people in our immediate physical areas, and at best those who are geographically accessible by whichever forms of transportation — walking, then carriages, then boats, then planes — were available (and affordable) to our ancestors at their respective points in history.

We also had written communication to extend our ability to communicate beyond our physical presence, both to another person in our time period, as well as to future generations. Consider though that until relatively recently in human history, the ability to read and write was restricted to a privileged few. In 1820, just twelve percent of the world's population was literate. There were some early outliers such as England and the Netherlands, those great colonial powers; by the mid-1600s just over half of their populations were literate on average (a statistic which hides a large gender literacy gap between men, the majority of them at the time literate, and women, mostly illiterate).[47]

In the late 1830s there came the telegraph, followed by the telephone several decades later, which was slowly adopted by developed nations during the early 1900s, finally becoming present in the majority of American homes by 1947.[48] The first transatlantic phone call, from the US to the UK, occurred in 1927. Millennials like myself, born following the 1984 breakup of the AT&T Corporation's monopoly over the Bell telephone system likely do not recall a time when landline calls outside one's local area were charged by the minute. Ergo, prior to this most working class people making a call any sort of real distance away had best have had something important to communicate in order to justify the charges.

While the letter and the telephone extended the reach of our communication abilities to another individual or group, these were still highly analogous to face-to-face communication. Note that in most cases when writing or calling, one had already made the prior acquaintance of the recipient. The average person's sphere of influence to share their thoughts was thus still restricted to a small or moderate social circle, just no longer gatekept by the limitations of who was within their immediate physical presence.

Contrast this now with the ability to *project* one's voice to a wider audience. Surely humanity came up with great developments in this regard as well prior to the internet. Books (made even more feasible by the printing press), plays, records and radio, movies and television... all of these provided a medium either for authors to directly convey thoughts and ideas, or allowed an artist the creative liberty to weave those elements within a story. Most importantly, these were effortful productions. Only a minuscule fraction of the humans that have ever lived have written a book, drafted a screenplay, recorded an album, or scripted a radio show. This has held true even over the past century, a period where the western world boasted incredibly high literacy rates which have risen to nearly one hundred percent today.

I will postulate a few reasons for this. First, creating content requires having something to say which one considers worth sharing with a wider audience, and also can eloquently translate into as few or as many words as required to convey such thoughts and ideas effectively to their reader, viewer, or listener. At the risk of sounding like a crass elitist, the average person is simply bland — a result of a life spent pursuing conformity — and has precious few thoughts or observations of any cogent novelty.

Second, creating content requires time, effort, and focused

discipline. As history has marched on, the luxury of such free time and the education and tools required to harness one's thoughts have become less and less the realm of a wealthy, privileged few and have trickled down to the everyman. Countless are the examples of authors and artists who have finished works while holding down a job and raising a family. Prolific fantasy author Terry Pratchett had a rule that he needed to write at least four hundred words every calendar day, no matter how tired he was from his day job. Though many people have a plethora of free time in the modern day, they either lack a task that they feel is worth contributing to humanity's cultural catalog, or have some idea that they never quite see through due to a deficit of self-discipline.

Third, successful projection of one's voice through creating content requires the resulting product to be impactful. Anything that is not profound, interesting, or entertaining will generally not be recommended or spread, and end up quickly discarded to the dusty annals of history. Those who have surpassed the first two hurdles may find a fate worse than criticism, which is that of their thoughts and ideas not being received at all.

Fast-forward to the present day, where the internet via social media platforms has upended yet another historical paradigm. No longer is the ability to project one's thoughts and ideas to a wider audience restricted to those who undertake the journey to create something effortful. These platforms have tapped into our desire to share and be heard, but have also broken social interaction down into its most base components in an effort to widen their appeal, more easily measure "engagement," and keep us hooked with a steady drip of validation and dopamine.

A Twitter post today (for non-paying users, at least) has a maximum length of 280 characters, which was increased from the previous limit of 140 characters in 2017. This resulted in the average "tweet" going from about seventy to eighty-five characters, and the number of posts within three characters of the limit went from 4.73% to 0.48%[49], meaning users were ten times less likely to hit the character limit when it was doubled. The sentence that you are reading right now is the same length as the average tweet. It's all part of an intentional design to keep users coming back multiple times per day, sharing bite-sized thoughts and the smallest developments of their life, in order to maximize the amount of time they spend on the platform.

In 2014, Reddit user "r_s" analyzed the average character length of comments in one hundred different subreddits. The average comment length ranged from around fifty characters at the low end, to around eight hundred at the high end for a subreddit focused on writing. Across all communities analyzed, the average Reddit comment length was about two hundred characters, nowhere near the site's limit of ten thousand characters. Is the typical piece of content on these platforms even long enough to convey meaningful thoughts and ideas?

Henry David Thoreau wrote in *Walden*, "Society is commonly too cheap. We meet at very short intervals, not having had time to acquire any new value for each other... Certainly less frequency would suffice for all important and hearty communications." When Thoreau wrote those words around 1846, the telegraph had been invented, but not yet the telephone. He was clearly writing about face-to-face communication, but it's abundantly clear what Thoreau's thoughts on social media would be if he believed that less frequent communication was the key to valuable human interaction.

As I mentioned earlier, ubiquitous smartphone access has democratized access to the internet, which in turn has democratized access to platforms which allow one to project their voice to a wider audience — sometimes friends, sometimes acquaintances, sometimes complete strangers. And this free access to these platforms, the simple *ability* to project one's every thought and opinion to an audience, it slowly warped into these users feeling *entitled* to do so. It used to be that you had to do something to earn a voice. Now everybody is holding a veritable megaphone — regardless of how misinformed, emotionally unstable, or uninteresting they are.

Far too many of us have been caught up in the arrogance and self-importance of playing the main character that we never stopped to ask whether we actually needed access to an audience of the size that the internet can provide. Does the average person really have that much of value to say that they require near-constant access to a platform to project from? I'd guess not, or else far more of us would have written a book, started a podcast or a video channel, published music, maintained a blog, or pursued any number of mediums which are more appropriate for what we consider important ideas rather than allowing them to be mixed in with dog photos, silly memes, and political rantings on our social media platform of choice.

The other side to sharing is receiving. And in the ceaseless grind of personal enlightenment and the overall progression of humanity, identifying and extracting the value contributed by those who have come before us is paramount. Anyone who claims to be a completely self-sourced fountain of profundity is likely a charlatan and a plagiary.

I have argued at length thus far in this book about the flaws of Reddit, making my case that the site is full of low-effort entertainment and oft-incorrect statements made by uncredentialled, argumentative users. Reddit is not a place to go to receive anywhere close to the best thoughts and ideas that humanity has to offer, rather just a place you can go for cheap amusement and to see what some random nobody thinks about various topics. That conclusion extends to every social media platform. Mentally, they're junk food.

Several users of Reddit's /r/NoSurf subreddit, a community of people focused on wasting less time surfing the internet, have expressed concerns about whether they've been negatively affected by these hypershallow social connections that Reddit has enabled. After doing some introspection, one user reports that they realized they were letting random peoples' opinion cloud their perspective on topics before they could even digest these ideas at their own pace. A twenty-year-old who claims to spend eight to twelve hours per day online reached out for help, titling their post, "Does anyone else feel like they have no personality or own opinions because of internet addiction?"

I must admit that I was caught in this trap for a long time before I recognized it during my own journey to disconnect myself from Reddit and other mindless web browsing in order to live more intentionally. I would read an article and immediately head to the comment section either on Reddit or the article itself to see how other people were reacting to it. After watching a video on YouTube, straight to the comments. Upon finishing a piece of media like a movie or television series, I would often seek out opinions and interpretations of it online before even coming up with my own conclusions.

As I began the first of my attempts in quitting Reddit cold turkey, I noticed that I had never actually lost the ability to form my own opinions, I had simply been short-circuiting it by tapping into social media and its endless cacophony of other peoples' thoughts. I began to use some of that time that I was no longer spending on Reddit to instead just sit and reflect about the information that I had received. I found that not consuming information rapid-fire as one does on aggregator sites like Reddit resulted in times of "boredom" returning, and it was during these periods when my mind was free to wander and reflect that I would come up with thoughtful conclusions of my own.

An almost obtusely existential line of questioning kept rising to the forefront of my mind. To what degree are we as individual people being changed by exposing ourselves to the thoughts of countless anonymous others on the internet, often in highly polarized hive mind communities? If the price for finding our "true" selves is disconnecting, is there any hope for this experiment going mainstream, or would most people consider giving up their social media to be too costly?

At some point, I had lost something valuable — most of what constitutes one's ability to think for themselves — and in a stroke of irony I was only best able to understand *why* upon consuming the words of another. In Cal Newport's *Digital Minimalism*, I highlighted the following passage: "As Kethledge and Erwin explain, however, solitude is about what's happening in your brain, not the environment around you. Accordingly, they define it to be a subjective state in which your mind is free from input from other minds." Newport goes on to argue that due to the omnipresence of our internet-connected smartphones, most of us have effectively completely banished any periods of solitude (and thus its benefits) from our lives.

I would caveat the above definition of solitude and instead say it is a state in which your mind is free from *active* input from other minds. It is perfectly acceptable to spend time ruminating on information that you have received from others and seeing where that train of thought takes you. This allows for the aforementioned recognition that we as a species progress by building upon the best contributions of our predecessors and contemporaries. One could certainly, for example, go to the woods and perform an experiment in living deliberately, however first absorbing Thoreau's account of his two-odd years at Walden Pond and then reflecting on those chapters before embarking could arguably provide one with a deeper experience.

I find that when reading books, I will often take short mental breaks from the page to process passages which I find to be particularly impactful. These snippets of solitude have value, and they are something that I almost never experienced in my time on Reddit. I think that may be a combination of the fact that little I was reading on the site was of real value, plus the fast-paced, all-you-can-eat buffet style of social media in general. As I rediscovered reading books after a decade spent consuming mostly Reddit posts and comments, I realized that the difference was in savoring. You cannot savor social media; it is antithetical to the sites' designs, and the concept of *creating* things which can be savored simply becomes lost on users of these sites over time, just as it did for me.

There's something to be said for spending one's media consumption time engaging with a single stream of focused consciousness at once, as opposed to dipping into a rushing river filled with the disjointed opinions of hundreds of anonymous strangers. A quality article from a passionate, knowledgeable subject-matter expert is perhaps worth a week or more of evenings spent trawling Reddit. A single good book, in my experience, can have more value than years of free time spent in "knowledge" forums online dedicated to the same topic.

Social spaces on the internet have become an overwhelming miasma of noise, with countless overlapping voices projecting their unfiltered stream of thoughts out into the digital ether. But just because they're broadcasting, does not mean that we have to tune in. We can ignore them, and go back to the way it was before. They say that we are the company we keep. The creators of the thoughts and ideas that we choose to consume surely rank among our company, even if we have not met them. Seed your mental garden from only the most thought-provoking, inspiring sources. Solitude is your water; contemplation a nurturing force. Implement this change in lifestyle, and you may be surprised what fruits are borne.

Chapter 13
What Reddit Stole From You

Perhaps surprising to those who do not study the discipline, economics is not just about money. Rather, it is the study of how humans make choices under conditions of scarcity. Economics is about decisions — people weighing various choices or alternatives — and the result of those decisions. Some of those choices involve money, but many do not.

As an economics nerd, I frequently go about my day thinking about things in economic terms. We all go through similar thought processes, whether one knows the proper jargon or not, because much of the terminology in economics was created to describe behaviors that we humans tend to engage in. There is an entire sub-field of the study known as behavioral economics, which developed based on the realization that decisions that people make in the real world often differ from the rational decisions that would be implied by classical economic theory. Learning to think like an economist has helped me to identify those situations, take a step back to observe my own thoughts, and ultimately make more informed, optimal decisions.

Arguably the most useful concept in economics is that of opportunity cost. In simple terms, it's the idea that when you're presented with multiple choices and must pick only one, you are losing the potential gain from the alternative choices relative to the one that you selected. A basic monetary example of opportunity cost is how you choose to allocate the money that you have left over at the end of the month after paying all of your bills and expenses. You could leave it sitting in your checking account earning zero interest, or you could invest it in a stock market index fund, let's say expected to earn a five percent average annual return after inflation. In this scenario, one hundred dollars today would have the purchasing power of $128 in five years; $163 in ten years; $265 in twenty years; $432 in thirty years. If you leave your money in the zero percent interest checking account, the potential profit that you missed out on by not investing your money is the opportunity cost of that decision. Likewise, by investing the money, you are losing out on having easily-accessible funds in your bank account and exposing yourself to a risk of it declining in value.

Just as with most things in economics, the concept of opportunity cost goes far beyond money. Remember, this is the study of how we make choices under conditions of scarcity. Using Reddit, other social media platforms, and time-wasting websites comes with several opportunity costs. I phrased this as "stealing" in the title of this chapter due to the manipulative ways in which these platforms capture our attention and attempt to squeeze ever more of it from us. This final chapter in Part I of this book will serve as an elucidation of the price that you pay for using Reddit and similar sites.

One of our scarcest non-renewable resources is time. For the proper perspective, we need to consider that for most of us who are not wealthy enough to forgo a traditional career, one's actual amount of free time left in the day is really quite small after doing all the prerequisite activities to sustain our lives. These basic tasks include things like sleeping, maintaining hygiene, working, commuting to work, preparing food, and various household chores. Some people consider exercise a necessity that must be allocated for. Those who have children must spend some time caring for them.

After performing all of these basic functions, most working age adults likely have just two to five hours of time on each weekday (depending on the various lifestyle choices they have made) that is *truly* free to use as they please. In technical terms a day is twenty-four hours, but in practical terms it can't be for anybody, since every human requires some amount of sleep.

It is a true statement that choosing to spend an hour scrolling social media is consuming a little over four percent of your twenty-four-hour day. However, leaving the analysis at that vastly understates the impact of that decision. When it's an hour out of your two to five hours of free time on a weekday, that is a much larger percentage. If that hour of scrolling on Reddit each day is costing you twenty to fifty percent of your free time, isn't that far more alarming?

Nearly every decision that you make with your free time comes with an opportunity cost. There are always many other things one could be doing during that same block of time, and many of us don't seem to have enough free time to do all of the things which we would like to. An ideally optimized day would see us concentrating our time into what we consider as the most necessary and important activities to our immediate survival and well-being, as well as long-term goals.

Whether time we have spent is time wasted depends on whether we are truly satisfied with the outcome. That is for us only to decide, and not for others to tell us. In any given day, are you truly content with how you spent your free time, or are you regretful that you did not use it in some other manner? Are you utilizing your days in a way that brings you contentment and satisfaction? Or do you have goals and dreams that remain unfulfilled while you scroll on your phone or computer, or undertake some other low-effort activity?

Have you ever done *anything* in life and thought to yourself, "I wish I had that time back so I could have spent it on Reddit, TikTok, or some other social media platform"? After learning a new skill? After exercising? After watching a highly acclaimed movie? Perhaps after going to the dentist, but is that really the bar that we want to set for the value of the activities to which we are choosing to give our time?

Don't get me wrong, I'm not implying that leisure time is bad by any means. You don't have to be productive during every waking moment, and anybody who claims that they are is either abusing stimulants or has some sort of course subscription to sell you. What I am asserting is that Reddit and similar sites that serve content on an infinite scroll are simply the lowest quality of information and entertainment around. Oftentimes, like in my case, we *acknowledge* that these sites don't serve us, but continue to use them due to years upon years of these sites worming themselves into our brain's reward pathways. Through that mechanism they are able to steal our attention away from other activities that we'd much rather be doing but which require a larger amount of activation energy.

Closely linked to time is another opportunity cost, that of your attention. Why shouldn't you be more selective of how you give access to your attention out? Would you let the top television watchers in your neighborhood by hours consumed per day come into your house, turn on your television, and choose all of your programming for you? Or worse yet, would you let some algorithm schedule your entire day for you? Why, then, should we cede these liberties to some faceless social media platform that is trying to make a buck off of our finite resources, and rewarding us in return (at best) with low-value entertainment?

By posting and commenting on Reddit, you are creating content for Reddit, Incorporated for free, which they then monetize. You could be using this time to start a website, write a book, begin building a small business, or learn any number of gratifying and enriching hobbies... All activities where you own and potentially benefit from the fruits of your attention, time, and effort.

In Chapter Eight, I estimated Reddit's annual Average Revenue Per User at just $2.67 in 2020. In Chapter Two, I made an inference that the average Redditor spends about a half hour daily on the site. Converting these two metrics into an hourly rate, assuming they are correct, shows that Reddit profited about 1.5 cents per hour off the time that users spent on the platform in 2020. This is all your time is worth to Reddit, Incorporated — a pittance — primarily because that is all that it is worth to their advertisers. I'd wager that any human alive today values their time at least an order of magnitude more than one and a half US pennies per hour (in September 2022, *The World Bank* updated their global poverty definitions such that the threshold for "extreme poverty" was set to $2.15 per person per day[50]). An interesting way to look at this is to ask yourself what you would pay to have a twenty-fifth hour in each day to use any way that you pleased. Peoples' answers would likely be all over the board depending on the value of their labor and their financial means, however it doesn't seem that anyone would willingly place as little value on their own time as social media platforms like Reddit do.

Another opportunity cost of using sites like Reddit is that of your mental energy. In my own experience, I found the process of using Reddit for extended periods of time to bring a certain level of mental taxation. Browsing posts and comments on the site brings a deluge of eclectic, disparate information, throwing one's thoughts every which way incessantly. Writing comments online — assuming that one cares about writing *understandably* in such an environment — demands at least attempting a coherent presentation of one's thoughts. Perfect spelling, grammar, and organizational structure are certainly not required in informal online interactions; commenting on Reddit certainly took far less mental energy than writing this book.

I often wondered whether some of the users who wrote terse comments full of mistakes had the capability to write well, but simply chose not to donate that level of effort to the likes of Reddit and its users. If that is indeed the case, I admit to jealousy of their pragmatic ability to use Reddit in such a selfish and one-sided manner, spending mere seconds to ask a question that another user might spend fifteen or twenty minutes answering, and never returning that effortful contribution to the community. So little of what is discussed, argued about, or presented on that site is of any real consequence, although those doing the discussing and arguing often think that they are doing a great service not only to their fellow user, but also to mankind. Personally, I am opposed to the mindset of selfishness in online interactions (despite recognizing the practicality of adopting it) because it encourages a tragedy of the commons scenario which disagrees with my idealized concept of the internet as a high-quality informational resource.

It takes mental energy not only to interact with other users, but also simply to parse replies to one's comments or posts and decide if we *should* interact with them. For example, when receiving a notification, you cannot know if the nature of it is trolling or insulting until you have already begun to read it, and by then at least part of the intent has been met. The message was delivered; even if you discard it quickly and refuse to engage, the troll was still able to occupy your mental space and energy for a period of time. Let alone the amount of energy that must be expended should one choose to genuinely defend their views and opinions against the frequent aggressive detractors that seem to concentrate on Reddit. The only surefire way to avoid these negative actors is to refuse them any point of access to you by not posting or commenting on social media platforms at all.

Finally, as we examined in the previous chapter, Reddit and similar social media platforms which are accessible from anywhere via our smartphones have stolen nearly all periods of solitude from many of our lives. The compulsion to use these sites and apps has filled in any potential periods of silence or self-reflection — colloquially referred to as "boredom" these days. It wasn't until I began to think critically about my usage of Reddit that I examined my own habits and realized how frequently I was filling small gaps in my day with scrolling on my phone. When at home with a few or more minutes between obligations I could access Reddit from multiple devices; outside the house whenever I had a spare moment such as standing in line at the store or waiting for someone to arrive I would pull out my smartphone and head straight to Reddit. Reddit of course is not everybody's social media platform of choice, however it seems that nearly everyone has *some* site or app they are engaging in a similar behavior with these days. Even many people of older generations who initially derided younger folks' propensity for smartphone addiction seem to have gotten sucked in.

I was born in 1993, at the tail end of the millennial generation, and more importantly one of the final birth years whose cohorts would have any distinct memories of a pre-internet era. I believe that I first used a computer around age eight, during the period when computers were still primarily viewed as professional tools and social media had not been invented yet. Young adults coming of age today likely do not recall a time when smartphones, social media, and connectedness were not ubiquitous. As a result, depending on whether they grew up in a household that imposed technology restrictions, some likely do not have any experience with true solitude or silence at all.

For me personally, regaining periods of silence in my life by cutting myself off from Reddit and other time-wasting websites that I turned to at the slightest hint of having unoccupied time has been overwhelmingly positive. A few minutes of silence offers a time to put one's thoughts in order, gain mental clarity and focus, ruminate on long-term creative projects, or simply enjoy a moment of peace. It presents the opportunity for self-discovery. I did not realize that I had forfeited all of these potential moments in my life until I began my first attempt to quit Reddit and other time-wasting websites for good. I was only able to rediscover the benefits of silence after blocking Reddit on all of my devices so that I could not habitually navigate to the site during moments of downtime. By doing so, I forced a reconciliation with my own thoughts.

Arguably, I was addicted to using Reddit, which is just one particular flavor of the digital addictions plaguing many people these days. Nearly everyone seems to have one or several websites and apps that they incessantly cycle their attention between, amplified by the omnipresence of our smartphones. How did we get that way? There are of course many factors: these platforms are inherently designed to be addictive so that we spend as much time as possible on them; perhaps a desire for escapism; a societal obsession with productivity manifesting as the desire to be constantly doing *something* even if that activity is wholly inconsequential.

I suspect that introverts like myself in particular may be more drawn to Reddit specifically compared to other social media platforms. The pseudonymous nature of the site lends to an inherently weaker form of social interaction than one gets from using other social platforms where the users are personally known to oneself, such as friends and acquaintances. This shallow level of social interaction may be pleasing to introverts, but paradoxically this is the same group that likely benefits the most from having occasional periods of true solitude in their lives, and if that is the case they would stand to suffer the most damage from overuse of these platforms.

Your time, attention, and mental energy are precious commodities, and are some of the major opportunity costs that come with using Reddit. In the vast majority of the chapters in the first half of this book, we examined criticisms and flaws of Reddit to present the argument that the site is of low or even negative value to its users. These last two chapters have focused more on the tangible downsides to those who continue to use Reddit and other time-wasting websites, in order to lay the framework for what you serve to regain by quitting these sites.

In some cases, such as my own, the addiction to Reddit and similar sites can be so severe that it robs us of the ability to live our ideal lives — constantly shelving and procrastinating things that we'd prefer to be doing in favor of cheap and familiar dopamine hits. Ridding myself of Reddit and all the detriment that it brought and instead using that time and energy to accomplish my goals has led to greater life satisfaction and a general feeling of contentment. If you're persuaded that quitting or severely reducing your use of Reddit is at least worth a try, the next step is to discuss how to approach and overcome what for many of us will amount to quite a difficult task.

Part II:

How to Quit Reddit
(And All Other Time-Wasting
Websites and Apps)

Chapter 14
"I'll Do It Tomorrow"

If procrastinators across the globe had a universal anthem, it would likely be "I'll do it tomorrow." Many people who struggle with self-discipline, motivation, or addiction fall into this trap. Whether it's someone trying to quit smoking or drinking, attempting to start a new diet and exercise plan, or trying to cut down on wasteful web browsing, many people seem to fail at these tasks (and quickly) while only a determined few succeed. Inertia being what it is, taking that first step in reforming habits can be the most difficult.

In terms of internet use, what does this procrastination and failure to change one's habits look like? It's a cycle of squandering a substantial portion of a day's free time — opportunity — browsing the web, then feeling regretful likely right before bedtime. An internal commitment is made to use one's time more productively tomorrow, however upon waking the next day, one of the first actions performed is checking in on our social media platforms or websites of choice. That evening, a commitment will be made to seize tomorrow *for sure*, and the cycle will continue ad nauseam. It is certainly mentally draining.

I know this cycle of digital addiction well because I have

been through it and successfully broken out of it twice, first with video games and then with Reddit, both of which I invested a large portion of my free time into until my late 20s. I use the word "addiction" not as a hyperbole, but because I truly believe that is an accurate assessment; for many years I wasn't truly enjoying the video games that I was playing, but was continuing to do so out of compulsion and habit. As I reported in the first half of this book, I wasn't getting much enjoyment or value out of most of the time that I spent on Reddit, either. Why did I continue dedicating my time to these activities long after I had realized they were unfulfilling? Surely there were more enjoyable ways that I could think of to fill my time!

One obvious explanation is that both of those activities are *designed* to be addictive, weaponizing our own psychology against us and exploiting our brain's wiring for the designer's benefit. Reddit and other social media platforms are optimized to extract as many minutes per day from as many users as possible, because that translates linearly to more advertisement revenue. Modern online video games similarly have a desire to take as much time per day from as many players as possible to maintain their game's relevance and popularity, which ensures that the players who purchase "loot boxes" for cosmetic items will continue doing so (as microtransactions and digital gambling have proven to be a far more lucrative model in the long run than designing and selling video games for a flat, one-time price). Exploiting any competitive advantage to its maximum degree is of course expected human behavior, and the businesses creating these products are owned by and run by humans.

But baked-in addictiveness isn't the whole story to why people like myself continue investing time into unsatisfying activities. Anyone who has sat through an introductory physics lecture has likely been introduced to Isaac Newton's Laws of

Motion, and probably knows that Newton's first law describes inertia — a body at rest remains at rest, and a body in motion remains on its path unless acted upon by a net external force. Colloquially, inertia describes a tendency to resist change, and long after Newton's time this concept has moved beyond physics and into the realm of psychology.

Psychological or behavioral inertia is the propensity to keep performing a behavior that one is already doing. It describes humans' tendency to maintain their status quo unless compelled by a significant psychological motive to intervene or reject it, which can manifest as individuals persevering in making suboptimal yet familiar choices.[51] Behavioral inertia can describe why it's hard to shut down a video game and go perform a more productive and rewarding activity, yet it can also account for the persistence of positive habits like engaging in regular exercise.

Writing on behavioral inertia in his book *Thinking, Fast and Slow*, psychologist and Nobel Prize-winning behavioral economist Daniel Kahneman hypothesized, "A general 'law of least effort' applies to cognitive as well as physical exertion. The law asserts that if there are several ways of achieving the same goal, people will eventually gravitate to the least demanding course of action. In the economy of action, effort is a cost, and the acquisition of skill is driven by the balance of benefits and costs. Laziness is built deep into our nature."

If you don't have a specific goal for how to spend your free time in the evening after work and on the weekends, then you will choose the path of least resistance. We are surrounded with easy, low-effort ways to pass time which include things like watching television, scrolling on the internet, and playing video games. The issues with these activities begin when they become our default way to fill unallocated time — recall that once our status quo is set, upsetting it requires a significant motive.

I spent some time reflecting about other root causes for why I was spending hours per day playing video games and posting on Reddit, besides simply the desire to pass time. My conclusion was that playing competitive online first-person shooting games (which I was fairly skilled at) gave me the feeling of being accomplished at something and the satisfaction of victory over others. Gaming was a simple, low-effort way to obtain these feelings. I also reasoned that I was spending so much time reading and writing comments on Reddit because I enjoyed reading but was too lazy to pick up an actual book for years, and I had a desire to write myself but a fear of actually putting pen to page. Reddit was a low-risk way to write several hundred words per day about topics that I was interested in and publicize my thoughts on an ethereal, pseudonymous medium that had no link to my real self. Just as Kahneman suggests, I had gravitated towards the least demanding method of achieving these goals.

To realize our true potential, we first need to overcome our nature. This is no novel realization. Nearly two millennia ago, the Greek Stoic philosopher Epictetus is recorded (as transcribed by his student, Arrian) in *The Enchiridion* as proclaiming:

> What other master, then, do you wait for, to throw upon that the delay of reforming yourself? You are no longer a boy, but a grown man. If, therefore, you will be negligent and slothful, and always add procrastination to procrastination, purpose to purpose, and fix day after day in which you will attend to yourself, you will insensibly continue without proficiency, and, living and dying, persevere in being one of the vulgar. This instant, then, think yourself worthy of living as a man grown up, and a proficient. Let whatever appears to be the best be to you an inviolable law.[52]

Epictetus and his fellow Stoic philosophers in the Greco-Roman era asserted that the only thing in life that is truly good is virtue, and that practicing the four cardinal virtues — wisdom, courage, justice, and moderation — is both necessary and sufficient to achieving *eudaimonia*, a concept with no direct English equivalent but often translated as "happiness" or "flourishing." The only true evil is vice: actions or falsely held beliefs that corrupt the pursuit of virtue.

Perhaps the best known practice of Stoicism in the modern day is the dichotomy of control, the understanding of what is within and what is outside an individual's control. The idea is that we have power over our own thoughts and actions in this world, but little else. Everything else to the Stoics was an "external," such as health, wealth, and reputation. One should be able to rationally determine the value of such external things as they are encountered on a daily basis, but ultimately view them with indifference once these events pass the threshold of our own control, at which time it becomes pointless to worry about them. For example, it would be virtuous to invest a moderate amount of time and effort into fitness, however even the most physically fit individual can still develop an incurable illness. The latter event is among those that the Stoics would advise indifference to; one's time and energy is better spent on continuing to improve oneself rather than worrying about things that one cannot change. With this approach, anyone was able to achieve *eudaimonia* regardless of their life circumstances if they could simply master their own mind, even the crippled former slave Epictetus himself.

In the Greco-Roman era, philosophy was considered an art of living, hence being a "philosopher" meant simply being a person who practiced a certain way of life, which is different from the modern interpretation of a person who professes philosophical theory. Under the classical definition, any person has the potential to be a philosopher if they so choose. When the Stoics talk about the difference between philosophers and the "vulgar," they are respectively contrasting those who lead a principled life of self-improvement with people who futilely chase and lust after externals. As Epictetus phrased it in a passage of *The Enchiridion*, "The condition and characteristic of a vulgar person is that he never expects either benefit or hurt from himself, but from externals. The condition and characteristic of a philosopher is that he expects all hurt and benefit from himself."

Unquestionably, almost all people are "the vulgar" by this definition; it is the default state of humans and behavioral inertia works to maintain this imbalance. Only those who put real effort into thoughtful self-improvement can become philosophers. I think the Stoics could arguably be said to be referring not just to those who follow the principles of Stoicism, but rather generally referring to anybody who chooses to live intentionally and as a philosopher would, regardless of their exact ideology.

Over two millennia ago, these philosophers identified that the majority of people never realize their full potential or truly flourish in life. Today, such an observation still holds true. Civilizations have come and gone; technology has improved and elevated many aspects of our lives; nearly one hundred generations have passed since the Stoics. Yet at once both poignantly and unsurprisingly, the people that inhabit the earth are still just humans, beholden to the same general thought patterns and behaviors regardless of time or place.

Think of all the people that you personally know in this world. What percentage of them would you consider to be fulfilled in life, or at least somewhere on their own path towards becoming so? I would imagine it's quite small. Most people lead a mundane and unremarkable existence relative even to their own expectations. They spend a large portion of their time chasing after things like material goods, status, and jockeying for position on career ladders; these goals are often inconsequential and sometimes even self-antagonistic to their wellbeing. Then they spend their evenings gorging on cheap entertainment to keep their brain occupied *just* enough lest it incite a revolt at the absolute indignity of the life that they lead.

If you have role models in any topic, they are hardly superhuman. Most just had the self-discipline to harness their free time towards a specific goal, the willingness to take risks in life, and the commitment to keep pushing when they failed. Arguably, what many people write off as luck — and then use to conclude that another's results are irreproducible — is more often than not the preparation and expertise from the former behaviors *creating* an opportunity which one is then well-positioned to take advantage of.

It is my observation (and my own personal experience) that people who have a static or growing backlog of tasks they'd like to accomplish, skills they'd like to learn, or general goals they want to make progress towards nearly always do have the potential time, they just suffer from behavioral inertia and do not allocate it wisely. They need a motive, a psychological nudge to re-prioritize their own development over entertainment. To be sustained, however, it needs to come from an internal locus.

The honest truth of it is that as long as your actions are not harming others, nobody else cares how you spend your time. The natural consequence of such indifference is that your psychological nudge will likely not be coming from an external source. The commonplace and socially acceptable nature of digital addictions means that one can waste hours per day scrolling various online content without so much as a concerned word from a family member or friend because chances are, they're spending their evenings doing the exact same thing.

That leaves this journey of reforming one's digital habits — in a wider sense, defeating behavioral inertia and learning how to use one's time intentionally — as a purely self-managed endeavor. This of course presents a catch-22 for those with established time management and motivation issues, but it's the honest truth of the matter.

That's a lot of words to essentially advise one to "just do the thing," which at face value is so blunt and obvious an instruction as to be nearly worthless as advice. However, the eighteenth century English writer Samuel Johnson notes early on in his series of essays appearing in *The Rambler*, "it is not sufficiently considered that men more frequently require to be reminded than informed."[53] The most important truths are often those derived from similar situations which humans faced with such frequency in history that they have come to be ingrained in our common wisdom, yet this position of prominence can also cause them to be flippantly disregarded. Intellectual humility is the recognition of the former; wisdom is the inclination to apply these inherent truths; insight is usually no more than a well-regarded ability to repackage these conclusions in a context which is particularly relevant or interesting to a modern audience.

The process of quitting Reddit and similar time-wasting websites involves finding the self-discipline and motivation to clear two simultaneous hurdles: that of behavioral inertia, as well as overcoming the habits formed and reinforced by the baked-in addictiveness of these platforms. That combination makes it a tough bar to clear: a study performed in 2012 focusing on desire and self-control found that the most common desire experienced by participants (following those to fulfill basic bodily functions like eating and sleeping) was media use. The desire to consume media also occurred significantly more frequently than participants reporting a desire to use either tobacco or alcohol.[54] This does not necessarily indicate that consuming various forms of media is more addictive than those drugs — although some psychologists believe that to be the case with social media in particular — as the higher frequency may be explained by a lower percentage of the population using any form of tobacco and alcohol compared to essentially every person consuming media on a daily basis.

However, note that in the decade that has elapsed between the referenced study being performed in 2012 and this book being written, social media usage has exploded — data gathered by *Statista* of the average daily social media usage of internet users worldwide shows steady growth from ninety minutes per day in 2012 to 147 minutes per day in 2022, a sixty-three percent increase![55] The landscape of tactics being employed has also changed drastically with platforms engaging in ever more insidious social engineering of their users in an attempt to extract yet more time from their days and keep them locked in these digital dopamine prisons.

The following chapters will address the tactics and strategies that I used to successfully overcome my digital addiction to Reddit and similar time-wasting websites, while simultaneously defeating behavioral inertia in order to spend my time more intentionally. It's the methodology that finally worked for me after many attempts and failures in a process that ultimately took over two years to definitively say that I had met my goal. The lessons I can share, but the motivation to implement them and stay the course needs to come from you. The best instruction on motivation that I can give is to start right now; not tomorrow, not next week. Right now.

Chapter 15
Avoiding Self-Help Purgatory

An oft-spoken observation among Redditors is that a subreddit exists for almost any topic one can imagine, so it's really no surprise that there are a number of self-help communities that have established themselves on the site. There are dozens of communities claiming the mission of fostering motivation and discipline among their members, for example /r/GetMotivated is ranked thirty-fourth among the list of most-subscribed-to subreddits. Support groups have even popped up on the site for users battling addictions to vices like alcohol and video games, and as previously mentioned, the /r/NoSurf community is an online support group for people suffering from internet addiction. Just like with in-person support groups, people use these forums to share their stories and exchange lessons learned as well as words of encouragement.

/r/NoSurf is obviously unique in that it's a support group hosted in the very environment that is problematic for its users. The irony of this is not lost on some commenters, who compare it to hosting an Alcoholics Anonymous meeting at a bar. I would certainly not say that criticism causes the negatives to outweigh the benefits of the /r/NoSurf community to the point that it is entirely counterproductive — at the very least those who subscribe there have arrived at the stage of questioning their own habits, and many have further acknowledged that the amount of time that they spend online is problematic.

Users there have differing goals; the group's stated intent is "a community of people who are focused on becoming more productive and wasting less time mindlessly surfing the internet." To some, this means reducing the amount of time they're spending using the internet to seek out mindless entertainment. Others strive to eliminate wasteful browsing entirely, including quitting Reddit. Of course, this would mean leaving /r/NoSurf behind as well, since it is hosted on Reddit.

In any support group, frequent topics of discussion are personal setbacks and failures on one's journey. Commonly /r/NoSurf users will post confessions of their relapses with internet addiction, for example late on a Sunday evening a user may post that they wasted their whole weekend browsing the internet despite having better intentions for spending their free time. Some users admit to having been sucked back into the habit of scrolling for hours per day after doing well for weeks or months prior. Many people report a desire to take that final step and quit Reddit for good — deleting their account as a sort of symbolic triumph — but finding themselves compelled to return to the site and create a new account a short while later.

These stories reveal that an alarming number of people suffering from internet addiction appear to be stuck in a sort of self-help purgatory. They *want* to drastically reduce their internet use due to some negative impact it is having on their lives, but for various reasons they are unable to keep that commitment and fall into the classic addiction cycle of relapse and binging, over and over again. My own experience mirrors this; it took me over two years to completely quit Reddit for good from the point I had recognized that my usage of the site was out of control and stifling my other goals and motivations. I believe there are several reasons why those suffering from internet addiction (and Redditors in particular) experience these repeated failures at different stages of the process.

After acknowledging their issue of spending too much time online, a first step for Reddit users is often an attempt to use Reddit itself more intentionally. They will likely pare down their list of community subscriptions, keeping ones that are geared more towards hobbies and education and removing the subreddits primarily focused on entertainment. This approach does not solve any of the core issues with Reddit's design or insulate one from the negative aspects of Reddit's culture, and a user will still be able to scroll the site infinitely unless they reduce their subreddit list to an incredibly small number of subscriptions. After a time, the user will likely realize they are spending the same amount of time on Reddit as they were prior, and still gaining little or nothing of value from the site.

Sometimes users undergoing this subscription revamp will add several motivation and self-help subreddits into their feed. This is a bid to make their time on Reddit part of a productive endeavor towards reducing their total time spent online. Instead of using Reddit for entertainment and absorbing useless trivia, they reason that they can instead use the site to learn tips and tricks to provoke the sort of lifestyle change that they're seeking.

This is of course nearly exactly what these people were doing on Reddit in the first place, and they have just shifted the type of information that they are scrolling endlessly through. I referenced the concept of compulsive information seeking or information addiction back in Chapter One; the behavior of continuously collecting information but never actually doing anything with it. This is the mentality that Reddit and similar social media sites have conditioned us for to maximize the time that we spend on their platforms; the idea that whatever you're looking for or need right now — even an answer to a question that you can't fully articulate — could be the next item that you scroll past. It's not surprising that generations like mine who grew up mostly or entirely online end up falling back on that reflex.

Searching Reddit for lessons in spending less time on Reddit is an exercise in futility. I reasoned that while some of the answers to *why* I should quit Reddit could be found on the site, the knowledge of *how* to quit Reddit would not be found there. Anybody who had completed the process and truly discovered "the way out" by definition would not feel the need to return to Reddit in order to share and discuss it with pseudonymous strangers.[56]

The /r/NoSurf community is a self-help purgatory for those suffering from the classic combination of internet addiction and a lack of self-discipline. Users of online support groups typically find value in being able to instantly connect with help during a moment of weakness, for example a top post on the /r/StopDrinking community describes how the user is "posting instead of drinking." This action puts them further from their vice and adds the reinforcement of others who are on the same journey, hopefully helping them to short-circuit that impulse.

I have already touched on the ultimate irony of /r/NoSurf (and furthermore, any other online forum for internet addicts) which is that the act of engaging with that support group causes people to perform the very behavior that they've found problematic and are trying to stop. The alcoholic can use the web to tap into a community of people who are also "not drinking" at that very moment. Someone posting on /r/NoSurf gets responses from others who are actively browsing Reddit. It is not possible to use the internet to connect with people who are "not browsing," as those are mutually exclusive states.

By the time the internet addict has turned to an online forum for help, they've already crossed the threshold. That's not to say there's no coming back from it, that they can't close out the web browser after posting there rather than wasting the next several hours scrolling on the internet. But the neurological reward circuitry underpinning their addiction has already been activated. In terms of vulnerability to further engaging in that undesired behavior, it's analogous to the alcoholic saying they're just going to have one drink.

Once I learned that the information I was seeking would not be found on Reddit itself, I thought that I might find people elsewhere talking about quitting Reddit, perhaps on a personal blog or vlog, or better yet a more traditional offline medium like a book. I did find a few short blog articles about why people had left Reddit, but I felt there was so much more that needed to be said about a site where humanity collectively wastes tens of millions of hours on a daily basis, which myself and so many others had struggled to break away from. The idea for this book was born as a comprehensive offline tool for those seeking to quit Reddit, such that they wouldn't feel the need to seek more information on the internet.

You cannot overcome an internet or social media addiction by finding a better online space to hang out at. With the benefit of hindsight, I can say with complete confidence that visiting any online forums or chat rooms related to internet addiction or self-improvement is counterproductive once it passes the point of acknowledging that one has a problem and then deciding to take action. Avoiding the self-help purgatory on this journey will save you quite a bit of frustration and time.

Chapter 16
Delete Your Account?

An interesting topic of debate among those who are attempting to quit Reddit for good is whether to delete their account. Quite frequently on the /r/NoSurf community, Redditors make a final post announcing their imminent plan to delete their account, and the [deleted] tag that replaces their username shows that they indeed followed through with that action. However, no metrics exist to show what percentage of the users who deleted their account truly stay away from Reddit for good versus reappearing and interacting with the site some time later on a new account. Several /r/NoSurf users (including myself) report going through a cycle of deleting accounts as a step towards quitting Reddit, only to create a new one several days or weeks later.

I think there are some positive aspects to deleting one's account, but also some valid points that may merit keeping a Reddit account while trying to quit using the site. The most glaring flaw of account deletion is the idea that it's a panacea; that the act of deleting one's account will wash their hands of the site for good and cause them to never desire to return. Some people may truly be able to manage this feat, but for longtime heavy users of Reddit who visit the site multiple times per day the process will likely not be anywhere near that simple.

If you care at all about your accumulated karma score or your post and comment history on Reddit, you need to break that mental attachment immediately. A couple of years ago, shortly after deleting my original Reddit account with over a decade of accumulated history I made a new Reddit account for what I claimed was productive purposes (which was really just the start of my experience with self-help purgatory). I then submitted a post to /r/NoSurf titled "Your Account Is Not an Archive of Anything" with the goal of helping others work through letting go of their Reddit legacy, which I viewed as an important first step in quitting the site. The following is a relevant excerpt from that post:

> This is a little hard to describe, but I used to feel like there was this "image" I had to present on this site. Someone who was smart, witty, insightful, and interesting. To meet this goal I would spend hours per day in my favorite communities carefully crafting comments that fit that persona. I would then go back and review my comment history a few hours or a day later, and if something didn't feel right anymore or had gotten downvoted I would delete the comment. I was a creator and a curator.
>
> I believe all of this was under the misguided impression that my internet trail was some sort of legacy. That in five years, twenty years, a hundred years in the future after I'm dead, someone will stumble upon one of my Reddit posts. Maybe it's an internet archaeologist, or maybe just a random citizen trying to get a feel for the times. Either way, they'd surely see one of my comments, get the exact impression of my persona that I wanted to convey, then click on my profile out of a

desire to learn more.

Much like today people pore over the works of insightful historical figures like Marcus Aurelius, in my imagination so too would these people do that to my Reddit profile. "Wow, what a smart and insightful person, who was this person?" they might wonder while scrolling through pages and pages of comments.

Of course, it's all a delusion. Your comments, your karma, your activity on this site has little meaning to anyone but you outside of those fleeting interactions with other users. Who will likely never remember your username, see you again, or form any sort of meaningful connection with you. It's very likely this site will die one day, along with the majority of sites that archive Reddit content. Even if it was preserved, you're probably not as insightful as you think you are, and even then is that what you'd want your legacy to be, some contributions to a pseudonymous internet forum or some other social media site?

If that sounds similar to you, or if the thought of deleting your Reddit account and losing access to or "ownership" of that accumulated history gives you pause, that's all the more sign that you need to press that button. All of your content will still be there under the [deleted] user tag; you're not robbing anybody of potentially useful information by deleting your account. Nuking your entire account is a great way to forcibly break that mental attachment and begin the process of moving on with your life.

The biggest downside of account deletion for someone who is actively trying to quit Reddit is that users who navigate to Reddit but are not logged in are instantly directed to the /r/popular feed. This may make it easier to get sucked into infinitely scrolling through low-effort content if they impulsively open the site. However, account deletion alone is likely not a sufficiently effective barrier for people with a deep-rooted habit of participating on Reddit, since creating a new account is easy, free, and can be accomplished in just a few seconds.

I used to recommend to people trying to quit Reddit that they delete their existing account(s), and immediately make a new account with zero subreddit subscriptions. Since they would leave that new account logged in, it overrode the redirect to the popular feed. Once they arrived on Reddit they would land on a blank page with no posts (the mobile site would show a spinning Reddit logo but never load any content) serving as a last line of defense and a final reminder not to waste time browsing the site. This is still the case for desktop users who change their preferences to make "old Reddit" their default experience, but this behavior has changed for users who access the site through other means.

The above technique is no longer effective on "new Reddit" or on mobile devices. By nature of their design, every social media platform has a vested financial interest in getting each of their users to spend more time on their site. Time-on-site directly translates to more advertisements seen and more opportunities for users to interact with other platform revenue streams (such as purchasing Reddit awards). Your time is their money; my readers know this at this point. This is the concept behind "suggested content," that if it resonates with a user it will give them a reason to spend more time on the platform now and in the future, which likely would not have happened without that nudge. It's of course packaged and sold as a benefit to users — they're helping you *discover* things — but this concept taken too far overrides the user's autonomy in selecting content or their ability to self-limit exactly what they want to see from a platform and nothing more.

As an example at the time of this writing, if a Reddit user

who has less than three subreddit subscriptions opens the mobile site, they will instead be redirected to /r/popular. From my past personal experience, I remember being able to have a personalized feed on the mobile site even with just one subscription (your home feed simply consisted of recent content from that single community), so if this is not a long-running bug it is clearly an intentional change. Apparently Reddit, Incorporated feels that if you have not selected enough content for yourself on their platform that this cannot be an intentional decision on the user's part, and you are clearly in dire need of their forceful help in finding items to scroll through.

Moving into the future, it is my expectation that peoples' conscious freedom to decide exactly what information they want to consume — and how much of it — from these massive online platforms will continue to slowly erode. As we discussed in Chapter Eight, these sites are being slowly redesigned through careful testing to optimize for the amount of our time they can extract. Those seeking a "low information diet" as Tim Ferriss advised are increasingly being redirected to consume more. On the other hand, this manipulative behavior becomes more and more obvious to users of these platforms, and for some people it passes the tipping point towards deciding to completely opt out of these highly-optimized digital prisons.

Unequivocally, I think that account deletion is a necessary step for those trying to quit Reddit, as anyone who is not able to accomplish this step is demonstrating that they care too much about their worthless karma points and the accumulated history under their pseudonymous online avatar. Working through these feelings will be a key step in reclaiming one's life from internet addiction.

For those who primarily access Reddit via "old Reddit" on a desktop computer, for now I can still recommend the practice of creating a new account with zero subscriptions such that they will be presented with a blank home page upon loading the site. In my journey of quitting Reddit, this was very helpful to me as a reminder to myself to exit the site when I navigated there out of raw habit. However, as Reddit, Incorporated has demonstrated they can change how the site functions at any time which means that this trick is not future-proof. I fully expect that the option to use "old Reddit" will be discontinued entirely at some point. As such (and furthermore because this tip is useless for mobile users), those seeking to short-circuit their ingrained impulse to navigate to Reddit likely require a more comprehensive, enduring method.

Chapter 17
Site Blockers

I found that the most difficult aspect of quitting Reddit and other time-wasting websites was breaking my decade-plus habit of immediately and almost subconsciously navigating to these sites when I was procrastinating a task or when I was bored — and I mean "bored" as in the modern semantically drifted definition of not actively distracting my mind by consuming some sort of media. Chances are that wherever you are and whatever you are doing, you could be on Reddit or any other website or app within five seconds or less. Many of us work on computers where we are a couple mouse clicks or a few keyboard strokes away from being anywhere on the World Wide Web, and when we are not tethered to a desk our trusty smartphones are usually in our pockets or already in hand.

Landing on some time-wasting website or app essentially guarantees that one will lose at least a few minutes to it, and in some cases an hour or more. This ease of access and near-instant immersion means that the risk of relapse is high, as the most fleeting desire to dive into the internet can then be fulfilled through a subconscious sequence of motions. Willpower in many cases only gets one so far. In the classic cycle of addiction, the compulsion to use a substance grows during abstinence, overwhelming the individual's willpower long before the point at which it peaks and begins to decline as they overcome their dependency.

Behavioral therapists often advise that one of the most important steps in avoiding relapse is to dodge the preceding temptation. This involves identifying triggering situations and environments that would historically cause one to engage in the undesired behavior and separating oneself from those as much as possible. For example, someone trying to quit drinking alcohol may conclude that they often drink when getting home after a difficult day at work, therefore it would be wise not to have any alcohol in the house such that they can't immediately give in to that temptation. The extra barrier of driving to the liquor store requires thought and action beyond subconsciously engaging in a habitual behavior, and importantly adds extra time for reasoning to allow them to regain their willpower.

Unfortunately, going without home internet access is simply not a valid option for many of us who rely on it for work (especially with the rise in working from home arrangements in white collar professions), and as a tool in fulfilling our personal obligations or hobbies. I have heard from several former internet addicts who, in a desperate last-ditch effort to overcome their addiction, canceled both their home and mobile internet plans. To get online they must head somewhere with free Wi-Fi access like their local library or a café; throughout their days they commit to memory or record a list of specific tasks they need to accomplish that require the internet, and head to their access point once or twice per week to complete them. The physical separation, complete inability to browse at home, and required intentional planning forces them to reform their habits. I'd wager that most people who waste too much time online either need, or at least would prefer, to keep their home internet access and instead figure out how to use it as a tool.

Luckily, there are methods to build behavioral barriers and reform our habits without completely cutting the cord. One can simply block any websites that they are tempted to waste time on through a variety of methods; this can be done on a per-device basis or even across an entire home network. I found that using technology settings to block any access to Reddit and other time-wasting sites was a very effective way to short-circuit the impulse to habitually visit these websites. This was invaluable early on in the process of overcoming my internet addiction, for example the first day after installing a website blocker I tried to navigate to Reddit out of sheer habit approximately twenty times. I would then be redirected to a page informing me that Reddit was blocked, and I only lost a few seconds each time trying to open Reddit as opposed to many minutes. Site blockers helped me succeed in spending less time browsing the internet where willpower alone initially failed.

The most simple type of website blocker comes in the form of web browser add-ons or extensions that offer this functionality. I made use of LeechBlock by James Anderson, which is free and open-source; all the user needs to do is install the extension, then specify which websites to block and at what times. The user could for example configure the extension to block certain websites during times of the day when they are supposed to be working, allot themselves a set time limit per day to spend on these sites, pick sites to block 24/7, or some combination of these options for different sets of websites. In the event that support for LeechBlock ends at some point in the future, there are many browser extensions that offer very similar functionality. Some web browsers sync extensions and settings across devices, but you may need to individually install and configure your site blocker on each device that you use, in which case an export feature for settings like LeechBlock offers can make this task easier.

Perhaps a more comprehensive approach towards site blocking involves restricting access to these undesired websites across one's entire home network. This has the additional benefit of being more time-consuming and complicated than disabling a browser add-on or extension. Some models of internet routers offer the ability to blacklist certain domains, either as a specific function or as a component of a parental controls tool suite accessible through the router's administration console. Usually one can select which devices to apply the restrictions to such that in households with multiple people, one person who desires to prevent their personal devices from accessing certain websites is not also imposing these rules on everyone else. If your router has such settings available, this is a simple approach to blocking sites on one's home network which most people should be able to figure out how to set up.

Another network-wide website blocking solution is setting up a custom Domain Name System (DNS) sinkhole. I use the free and open-source "pi-hole" software running on a cheap Raspberry Pi single-board computer. DNS sinkholes like the pi-hole prevent requests to known domains containing advertisements, trackers, and malware from resolving, and are most commonly employed to prevent advertisements from loading on any devices connected to the network. This differs from the behavior of stereotypical ad blocker extensions which simply hide ads after they have already loaded; the custom DNS setup drops the request completely, helping to save internet bandwidth and reducing page load times, and additionally prevents other sorts of tracking activities outside of the web browser from being transmitted on your network. The pi-hole administrator can choose to blacklist certain websites in a similar manner to the router example described above, so for example one could prevent requests to www.reddit.com from resolving on specific devices, denying the site from ever loading at the network level. Setting up a pi-hole can be a fun and affordable little project that helps one learn a bit about computer networking.

The largest flaw of these website blockers is that if you are setting them up for yourself, naturally you will know how to reverse that process and disable them. They are therefore not a panacea in terms of never going on Reddit or any other undesired site again. A user with administrative rights (which most of us have on our own devices) could easily disable a website blocker extension in a couple of clicks or toggle off the blacklist of certain domains in their custom DNS settings.

It would be prudent to have realistic expectations in how one thinks these site blocking tools should be employed. They are there as a reminder and an extra barrier for you, to give you a mental prompt and the required amount of time to choose to regain your focus and commitment to live more intentionally after you have habitually navigated to a time-wasting website. For example, if I was writing and got distracted, then reflexively opened a new tab and tried to navigate to Reddit, my site blocker would interfere and I'd instead see a page served by the extension telling me that Reddit was blocked and would never be unblocked. This serves as my reminder that I opened Reddit out of sheer habit but shouldn't be on the site, and kick-starts the thought process that I should be writing instead. It's up to me to have the self-control to not bypass these additional barriers that I have set up for myself.

I personally had success with and would recommend employing multiple layers of site blockers. This can create a seamless experience between being at home or away, as well as provide a further deterrent towards disabling the blockers due to having to reconfigure multiple components. I set up a network-wide blacklist of time-wasting domains at home using my pi-hole, as well as installed site blocker extensions in the web browsers of all of my devices. When away from home a custom DNS sinkhole on the home network is no longer in effect unless one sets up a Virtual Private Network (VPN) routing through their home network, so in the situation of being connected to mobile data on my phone or a different wireless network my browser add-ons would continue to block these websites.

People who truly struggle with self-control may still not find such a setup to be sufficient. When the topic of site blockers comes up, many people attempting to overcome an internet addiction report disabling these barriers and relapsing to binge on scrolling through low-value content online. While this is ultimately a self-discipline problem that the individual needs to work through as discussed in Chapter Fourteen, one who is truly committed to changing their technology use habits but finds themselves disabling these site blockers can institute some escalating protections to make it more difficult to do so.

An interesting way to make web browser extensions more difficult to uninstall is to set up an enterprise policy on one's personal computer in the same manner that workplaces and schools do. In the Microsoft Windows operating system, users can use the Registry Editor to create a key for their preferred web browser which then forces a specific extension to remain installed and enabled at all times. The user will no longer be able to right-click to disable the extension, toggle it off from the browser settings page, or uninstall it. Linux and MacOS do not have registries, but the same outcome can be obtained through editing the browser configuration file. A word of caution: using the Registry Editor improperly can cause serious issues on your computer. Make a backup of your system and important documents prior to editing the registry, and potentially avoid tinkering around in there altogether unless you're reasonably certain of what you are doing.

There is one perhaps penultimate solution for anyone who proves to have so little self-control that they just cannot help themselves from disabling their site blockers despite wanting to make a lifestyle change. Once you have verified that everything is functioning properly, provide control of the administrative password to your router or DNS sinkhole to a trusted family member or friend. This will prevent you from modifying any settings on your own, most importantly the ability to remove time-wasting websites from the blacklist. If you need access for technical troubleshooting or some other reason, you can request the password from this person to do that one specific thing, after which they will set and record a different password. I have heard this method has worked well for those with an internet addiction so severe that they cannot stop browsing despite experiencing negative impacts on their life.

Setting up these site blockers was a vital step in my long journey towards successfully quitting Reddit. It was actually the final hurdle that helped me pass the threshold of not visiting Reddit for a month straight after over a decade of near-daily use of the site, when my previous attempts to quit had only lasted a few days to a couple of weeks. My site blockers acted as an additional barrier during moments of weakened resolve, providing a reminder and enough time for me to regain my commitment to change my technology habits. This could be just the tool that gives you enough assistance to meet that goal, too.

Chapter 18
You'll Never Scroll to the End

Quitting Reddit specifically is almost certainly what drove you to pick up this book. But you're also likely aware that the World Wide Web is a vast ocean of content, and even if Reddit were to go offline permanently, those tens of millions of daily users would disperse out into the digital ether and find new ways to waste the same amount of time online. Anybody who recalls using the site StumbleUpon during its sixteen years of existence before it shut down in 2018 can directly attest to that. Users would select topics of interest to them, then click the "stumble" button and be sent to a random webpage that likely aligned with their interests and which they almost certainly would never have found without the help of the tool. The randomized tranche of sites which StumbleUpon presented were for me a firsthand example of the utterly massive trove of content that existed on the internet.

Google currently claims that their own search index "contains hundreds of billions of webpages and is well over 100,000,000 gigabytes in size," and it's important to note that is *after* they've filtered out multiple times that number of sites due to identifying them as spam or low-quality content. Even if one could further personalize Google's index to only the sites and content that they would personally find interesting, considering that one-ten-thousandth of their index is still tens of millions of pages, I think it's safe to declare that even if one did nothing but consume online content during their waking hours that they would barely make a dent in getting through it during their lifetime. Of course, the internet continues to grow daily — and if more content that you'd be interested in is added than can be consumed in a single day, you'd be making backward progress. All that's to say that you'll never scroll to the end of the internet, but you *could* scroll until the end of your life.

The vastness of the web and near-instant ability to access any portion of it warrants a holistic approach to reforming one's online behavior. What you were doing on Reddit — scrolling, wasting time, reading things, shallowly interacting with other people and pretending to be part of a community — you can do a lot of places on the internet. One could be successful with the task of quitting Reddit but fail to overcome the behavioral inertia to defeat their underlying internet addiction and find themselves spending the same amount of time that they would sink into Reddit on an alternate low-value website, fundamentally changing nothing about their life. I spent the majority of this book sharing my thoughts and opinions about Reddit, but I thought it would be helpful to take a chapter to discuss my feelings about other common online pastimes.

Let's start with social media, into which bucket I will include sites like Facebook, Instagram, Twitter, and whichever new companies with similar concepts ultimately arise to replace them in the future, much as Facebook killed Myspace. While the use case for social media as a tool for actually maintaining relationships was always dubious at best, these sites are following the same trajectory as Reddit, continuing to decay and sell out their users' experiences while warping what these platforms were supposed to be in the name of increasing engagement and profits. Meg Watson authored an article for *The Sydney Morning Herald* in July 2022 titled "Why Your Friends Are Disappearing From Your Instagram Feed" which neatly diagnoses the issue; she writes that "Instagram was supposed to be a living photo album" with one's friends and family, but users' feeds have now been taken over by sponsored and recommended posts from "high-profile accounts, viral video creators and internet-famous dogs."[57]

We all know the common tropes of what occurs on each of these social media sites, which have arisen because they're mostly true; in the online debate of which social media platform is best, people usually vehemently defend their favorite platform of choice and pull the wool over their own eyes as to its shortcomings while accurately generalizing the negative aspects of every other site. Facebook stopped being cool years ago; for people in their 20s and 30s, it's now the site where their parents go to argue about politics and scroll through posts from people whom they mostly haven't genuinely interacted with in years. Instagram was the fill-in for younger generations for a while, but that's flopping now too. Twitter is where millennials and Generation X go to argue about politics, catch news updates and memes related to current events, and read bite-sized statements of the obvious posted by pop culture figures who really think that they're quite profound.

Much like Reddit, these social media platforms are all filled to the brim with crap and they're continuously getting worse. The main reason that I have heard people use to justify why they hang out on these sites is that they're using them to stay in touch with friends and family. But who are they interacting with on these sites that's supposedly an important person in their life, yet they don't have a phone number, email address, or alternate method of contacting them? No, the real reason people like these sites is that they offer an ultra low-effort way of *claiming* that you're maintaining a relationship with someone. But if you or they won't put in the effort to call, exchange texts, or meet in person every once in a while, is that really a relationship worth pretending to maintain?

I have a Facebook account that is mostly inactive (I say "mostly" because I upload a photo maybe once per year, and am occasionally tagged in a photo uploaded by someone else) with 421 "friends," which is a heck of a lot more people than I can actually count among my friends and family. Several years ago, when I was still occasionally using Facebook, I engaged in a practice of unfollowing people whom I wasn't keeping in contact with any longer whenever their posts would appear in my feed. The result was that the updates from most people whom I went to high school and college with but would likely never talk to again were purged from my feed, leaving a short list of posts from my actual friends and family. Amusingly enough, this broke the Facebook site; my feed had an "end" to it and whenever I would reach it the user interface would start spasming up and down, then the tab would freeze up in a futile bid to load more content when none could be found. I took this as a sign that one's feed wasn't *meant* to end, and that this was such an uncommon edge case that Facebook's QA team had stopped testing for it altogether. If you're going to continue using social media, I would recommend performing a similar purge of your "friends" list.

In a previous chapter, I discussed the pros and cons of deleting one's Reddit account for those attempting to quit the site. For other social media platforms, I believe that this is overwhelmingly a good idea for anybody who needs a nuclear option to cut down the amount of time that they are spending on these sites. Unlike Reddit, most social media platforms limit what content you can see without logging in. You don't get a personalized feed, and when navigating to a profile or page one is either completely restricted from viewing it, or is allowed to scroll only through a limited number of posts before getting a message that they need to log in to continue using the site. From a design and techno-philosophy standpoint I detest the registration wall, but it does a great job at keeping users who are not signed up from sinking any time into scrolling through the site if they go on just to check up on one or two specific things.

Another common online pastime is consuming curated video content. It differs from social media because the user is not primarily interacting with other users, but rather with the content. Platforms that fall into this category are YouTube and similar sites, and apps like TikTok — which according to multiple sources was the most-downloaded smartphone app worldwide in 2020, 2021, and 2022 (it came in second in 2019, losing out to WhatsApp by about a hundred million downloads).[58,59,60]

On my Android smartphone I have an app called ActionDash that monitors my screen time. A unique feature of the app is that you can see global average usage statistics using data collected from all users. At the time of writing in December 2022, TikTok had the highest average daily usage among all apps; ActionDash users with TikTok installed spent on average two hours and six minutes *daily* in the app! Clearly, the format of blasting people with a feed of short, algorithmically-curated videos has taken smartphone addiction to a whole new level. TikTok is mental junk food, and it's unlikely that one will learn or accomplish anything useful on the platform. It's a hotbed for the type of fake, staged, and scripted content that I discussed in Chapter Eleven, so even for amusement it's an incredibly poor-quality choice. One can argue that there are multiple facets and subgenres to TikTok that contain different types of content and they've found something useful on the platform before, but again we're back to the needle in a haystack analogy; I have yet to hear of a single person who uses TikTok for anything other than wasting ungodly amounts of time while swiping on their phone in a zombified state. The idea that one will wrestle with the algorithm to only show them valuable things seems antithetical to the app's design and a fool's errand.

I've taken to calling this structure "Random Access Media," because the users don't get to directly choose what to watch. Another testament to the addictive nature of this short-form media delivery content is that after TikTok rose to popularity in the western world, similar features rode in on its coat tails on other social media sites, namely Instagram Reels, Facebook Reels, and YouTube Shorts. They say that imitation is the sincerest form of flattery. It's also perhaps the easiest way to avoid losing your users — and the advertisement revenue that their attention generates — to competing platforms which have discovered a way to capture an even larger share of their time. Imitation is less risky than innovation. TikTok and its ilk pose a bigger threat to our personal time than any online website or app that has come before. In my opinion, these services have nearly zero redeeming qualities or potential value and one should delete or discontinue any use of them immediately unless they are one of the lucky few raking in boatloads of cash from these platforms (if this isn't already you, you're probably not going to make it as an "influencer").

YouTube is of course the most popular online video content delivery platform and where it differs is that there is objectively some valuable content on that site, and unlike Random Access Media one can directly search for what they are seeking. YouTube has a lot of value for finding tutorials for various tasks, especially for those who are visually-oriented learners. For example, you can watch a video of someone replacing the spark plugs on the exact model of car that you own, then follow along and learn the process yourself instead of mucking around with your car's included maintenance manual. There's a wealth of technical knowledge on YouTube, including college lectures. I used YouTube to complete Harvard's CS50 "Introduction to Computer Science" class which they've published under the OpenCourseWare initiative, accessible for free to anybody.

On the other hand, there's a lot of low-quality entertainment, incorrect information, and clickbait on YouTube. One could certainly use it as a "Reddit replacement" by getting sucked into an infinite stream of junk video content. One must be incredibly careful in curating what sources of information they will tune into on YouTube, for example, most videos on investing that I have seen on the site essentially amount to complete misinformation. I would suggest as a general rule that there is an inverse relationship between how often someone posts videos on the platform, and how important what they have to say is.

I believe that it's best to use video streaming sites like YouTube as a tool. My usual purpose for visiting YouTube is when I am in search of a solution to a specific problem that I believe will be better solved by visually observing someone else perform the same task, then I go see if such a video exists. There are several browser extensions that will remove all the distracting and "engagement boosting" features from the site. A few examples are Unhook, Distraction Free Tube, and Rabbit Hole for YouTube. These extensions do things like hiding the home screen feed, hiding the recommended video sidebar, and permanently disabling new videos from auto-playing when the current one finishes. Overall, they make YouTube much less addictive and I would recommend trying such an extension to anybody who has demonstrated the behavior of wasting too much time on YouTube.

Let's move to another common online pastime these days,

especially among the younger generations: chat apps such as Discord. Unless you are exclusively using these apps to occasionally chat with people whom you personally know in real life, these are decidedly even more worthless than Reddit. The rapid-fire nature of the chat format encourages low-effort contributions and the search function is mostly unusable, making knowledge archival difficult when the same is easily possible on forums or even Reddit. I know several people who spend time on Discord chatting in hobby-related servers and swear it's valuable, but they never seem to expand their depth of knowledge on these topics. Unsurprisingly, it turns out that they're using a chat app primarily for mindless chatter.

Worse yet are the people who hang out in online chat rooms or "Discord servers" and converse with people they don't even know in the real world almost continuously throughout the day. I once downloaded Discord — ultimately a mistake which I quickly rectified — because the developers of a game that I was playing at the time made it compulsory to have a Discord account to complete certain tasks in the game requiring coordination with other players. I poked around in the app for a bit and noticed the same few dozen people were sending most of the messages in the chat channels, and they'd pop on continuously throughout the day to do so. When I was discussing the purpose of the app with a younger coworker, he informed me that it wasn't uncommon for teenagers and young men to engage in this behavior of chatting with random internet strangers constantly during their day across multiple Discord servers, even considering themselves to have "online friends," a caveat to denote that they had never met the person in real life yet considered them a friend. I take issue with that concept, and furthermore, as someone who formerly spent a lot of time online I have my doubts that "internet people" are at all commonly well-adjusted enough humans to be worth investing in any sort of relationship with.

Let's pivot now to a different type of online communication method which actually has elevated to the status of being required in today's online world: email. There are not many digital services left that one can take advantage of without creating an account with an attached email address. For many of us, our primary email account is our most sacred account, and if compromised by a hacker would offer a gateway to nearly all aspects of our online lives including our finances. As a result of its preeminence, marketers consider a valid email address one of the most powerful pieces of personal information. If we are sent an email message that isn't flagged by a spam filter, it's highly likely we will at least read the title of the email. Every commercial service and company hungers for this level of access to consumers, and left unchecked the result will be an inbox that is utterly exploding with messages, requiring quite a bit of time each day to keep up with.

Anybody working in an office setting already deals with quite a bit of mandatory email each work day, sorting through a stack of emails in the morning by reading, responding, or deleting as necessary. The last thing that I find palatable is the idea of having to pay even a quarter of that amount of attention to my personal email account. Most people seem to give up and let their inbox become overwhelmed — nearly every time somebody has shown me their email account, I note unread messages numbering in the hundreds or more commonly thousands, and what looks like a flood of promotional emails from various retailers they had previously shopped at.

This was how I approached my email account for a while too, until one day I got fed up with the volume of email that I was receiving, which led to me occasionally glancing over actually-important items because they were lost in a sea of newsletters and notifications that some store's sale was starting or ending soon. From then on, I began a process of relentlessly unsubscribing from anything that came across my inbox that I would have otherwise deleted without reading. I didn't need daily marketing emails from stores that I shopped at once or twice per year. Any retailer sending me a daily email that didn't have an option to tone down to a weekly frequency, I unsubscribed from out of sheer principle. These days I get one to two dozen emails per day instead of well over a hundred. I only recently got out of the habit of leaving a web browser tab with my email account open all day, realizing that no email sent to my personal account has ever been truly urgent enough that it required me to quickly see and respond to it. Checking email twice per day is more than sufficient for a personal email account.

Finally, let's turn to one last digital pastime, the news. These days, plopping down in front of cable television news is an outmoded methodology of the baby boomer generation. In the digital world, people are mainly exposed to news through their primary social platforms — fifty-nine percent of Twitter users, fifty-four percent of Facebook users, and forty-two percent of Redditors reported regularly getting the news from those platforms according to the *Pew Research Center*'s "News Use Across Social Media Platforms in 2020" survey.[61] Nearly all users of social media sites get *some* news from them, as a fair amount of the content shared on these sites is based on current events. Even only occasionally clicking open the /r/popular feed on Reddit for example will keep one in the loop with at least the general theme of major events occurring in US and world news.

Inspiringly, people around the world are choosing to forsake tuning into the news more than ever before. According to a *Reuter's Institute* "Digital News Report" published in June 2022, forty-two percent of Americans (and thirty-eight percent of respondents across all countries) reported that they sometimes or often actively avoid news coverage, with a significant percentage giving the reasoning that they think the news contains too much politics, can't be trusted, or that it negatively affects their mood.[62] Additionally, a 2022 *Gallup* poll found that Americans' trust in mass media is near record lows. In 1976, seventy-two percent of Americans reported having a great deal or fair amount of trust in the mass media; that figure is just thirty-four percent in 2022. The percentage of Americans reporting having no trust at all in the mass media increased from four percent to thirty-eight percent over the same time period.[63]

For me, the ability to work from home brought about by the coronavirus lockdowns beginning in March 2020 meant that I wasn't listening to my local public radio station's morning news coverage on my twenty-five-minute commute into work, and quitting Reddit removed the other main way that I was hearing about breaking and ongoing news events. These changes eventually overlapping in the same time period caused me to totally disconnect from receiving "general news" coverage, and I've never felt like anything was missing in my day-to-day life. That's because my actions reinforced what I already knew (and most people know) prior to disconnecting from the news: that it's unactionable garbage and is thus a complete waste of time. I suspect that much like disillusioned Redditors, people who spend a lot of time keeping up with the news know that it's a low-value activity that is often detrimental to them, yet they continue to tune in out of habit and behavioral inertia. There's truth in the idea of being an informed citizen, but the myth sold to us by the mainstream media is that they're the purveyors of the valuable and correct information required to make us such.

In my experience, any big news stories you will hear about anyway through interactions with friends, family, and coworkers who are stilled plugged into the mainstream media. If you care about learning more at that point (which you probably don't) you can go look up more on that particular event. It's far more likely that you're personally interested in a particular facet or two of the news like the economy, and if this is the case you can put in the effort to find an online source or a podcast that provides non-sensational, informational coverage on that singular topic. This allows one to stay attuned to the particular segments of the news that impact or interest them while filtering out all the other rubbish that constitutes the majority of mainstream media coverage like political bickering and celebrity gossip.

There are innumerable ways to waste time using nothing but a web browser and an internet connection. Many people have opted to spend hours of their day passively consuming content online, yet continue to live a life that they are not completely satisfied with and let this activity which is ultimately of no value take priority over their responsibilities and aspirations. If one successfully quits Reddit but redirects all the time they were spending on the site into some other pointless website, they have not enacted a meaningful change. For some, reforming this surfing habit necessitates upending not just how we use the internet, but also how we approach the technologies that provide our gateway to the internet. We've allowed these devices to pervade our lives and incessantly blast us with notifications and instant-access temptation on the simplified assumption that what they provide is generally positive; *connection* is good, *information* is good, and one can never have too much of a good thing. As it turns out, that assumption was wrong.

Chapter 19
Redefining Your Relationship With the Internet

Quitting Reddit or any other websites or apps that you sink your free time into is one part of a holistic journey towards redefining how you interact with and conceptualize both the web and technology in general. Employing things like site blockers should simply be a short-term solution aiding you in realizing this paradigm shift. But what is the ultimate goal as to how we should ideally be using the internet and technology? We need to answer this question to know whether we have succeeded or not.

In an opinion article that appeared in *Frontiers in Psychology*, Alessandro Musetti and Paola Corsano argue that the internet is no longer a tool but rather an environment, and that this shift requires revisiting how internet addiction is defined. There is a historical premise of technological developments being introduced as a tool for a particular use case that end up driving substantial changes in peoples' behavior when they are used in ways other than initially envisioned, thus changing the very environment that characterizes our human experience. They note that "In particular, the criterion of 'heavier or more frequent use of the Internet than intended' lacks a comparative parameter in the environmental view of the Internet. How much Internet use is normal if the Internet is ingrained in every part of people's lives and also extends their cognition?"[64]

The argument presented by Musetti and Corsano is perhaps valid for scientists attempting to quantify as many variables in the world as possible in order to study it as a standardized system. For individual, actual people, though, I'll push back on the premise that "the concept of the Internet as a tool to connect to a virtual reality that is separate from the real world is no longer current." What if maintaining this viewpoint allows someone to live to their fullest potential? Such a person would be an outlier in a society where people are spending increasing amounts of free time online such that it is blending into reality and modifying the human experience. Psychologists must adapt their methodologies to the overall state of the world, but as individuals we do not have to conform to this new status quo.

Likewise, how much internet use is too much is up to the individual to determine. If someone who spends two hours per day online scrolling through low-value content wants to declare themselves as having an internet addiction due to experiencing negative effects in their life and observing compulsive behavior, that is for them to decide. Perhaps they will not be met with empathy from someone who spends more time online while engaging in enriching or educational activities that they value, and they may even encounter derision from others in denial about their own levels of internet use. You don't need to reach rock bottom or have some professional officially "diagnose" you with an internet addiction according to some academically agreed-upon definition before you are allowed to do something about it.

Redefining one's relationship with the internet starts by

critically examining how we use it. Answer to yourself the following questions — and I'd encourage writing down your answers such that you are forced to think about them:

1. How much time do I spend on each social media platform and time-wasting website or app per day? Be honest and add up all the small visits you make to these sites throughout an entire day. If you also access these platforms via your phone, the built-in screen time monitoring tools on your smartphone may help you figure this out.

2. What benefits am I seeing from my usage of these sites? If any, does this feel like a fair exchange for the amount of time that I spend on them?

3. Do I have unmet life goals, aspirations, or activities that I would rather be doing but never seem to find the time or activation energy for? What are they?

Remember, even thirty minutes per day on these sites can qualify as too much if it is interfering with other things that you would rather be doing. The goal of this activity is to quantify the amount of potential free time that you are losing each day to internet use that adds little or no value to your life. Again, be honest with yourself in filtering out the fluff. For example, if in a typical day you spend forty-five minutes on a particular social media platform and listed a benefit of it as "staying in contact with family and friends," does that activity really consume the full amount of time? Perhaps you spend ten minutes per day realizing this benefit, and the remaining thirty-five minutes scrolling through content from people you don't know or no longer talk to, low-value entertainment, or sponsored posts from brands.

If you're like I used to be, it's likely that the vast majority of things that you're doing online are not essential or meaningful. I'd wager this applies to most people who have internet access by this point; older generations that spent the first decade of widespread smartphone availability chiding youngsters for the amount of time they were spending staring at their phone screens have finally succumbed to technology addiction as both the devices themselves and the platforms they access have become easier to use. *Nielsen*'s Total Audience Report from 2021 shows that the age 50–64 bracket spent nearly three hours daily using smartphones and tablets to consume media and the age 65+ group spent about two and a half hours daily, compared to three hours and twenty-five minutes for the age 18–34 cohort.[65] As I suspected, internet addiction is now nearly ubiquitous.

The irony does not stop at the fact that our elders' smart-device usage has nearly come up to par with that of the youngest adults. It's that baby boomers were sermonizing about smartphones and early forms of internet entertainment all while being the most television-addicted demographic in American history — ultimately not surprising for a generation whose parenting style could likely be generalized by the phrase "do as I say, not as I do." Americans over age fifty are still spending nearly six hours daily watching television (a figure which includes both cable and streaming formats) compared to an hour and twelve minutes daily for the 18–34 demographic. Adding smart-devices into the mix has merged with their television habits into a sort of "dual media addiction" that has the oldest generations actually spending drastically *more* time per day in front of a screen than young adults. Both the age 50–64 and 65+ cohorts were reported by *Nielsen* as spending about nine and a half hours per day in total consuming screen-based media (obtained by subtracting out the reported time spent listening to radio), while this figure for the age 35–49 and 18–34 demographics was about nine and seven hours respectively. I was quite surprised to discover that the youngest adults actually spent the *least* amount of time consuming media each day, both in total and from screen-based sources.

Some may be inclined to write off these figures as older generations being more likely to be retired and thus having more time on their hands. This is certainly a large factor for the 65+ age group, but less so for the tail-end baby boomers and early Generation X. Q4 2022 data from the *Organization for Economic Co-operation and Development* shows an eighty percent employment rate for the 25–54 age bracket in the United States, which drops to sixty-four percent for US workers aged 55–64.[66] This reasoning also does not explain why the remainder of Generation X aged 35–49, solidly of prime working age, spends more time consuming media than younger adults. The answer is, again, television, which they consume less of on average than their boomer parents but still more than the youngest adult cohort.

The *Nielsen* report also reveals that accessing the internet via a computer is, on average, comparatively not a popular pastime. Across all age groups, this varied from a minimum of twenty-eight minutes to a maximum of forty-one minutes daily. I found this interesting because in terms of general use but especially for potential productivity, I have always preferred to be using a desktop computer (or at least a laptop), as I find the larger amount of screen real estate and a physical keyboard are both much more effective for accomplishing anything on an electronic device. Smartphones and tablets are ill-suited for little other than simple tasks or passively consuming content while lying around, which of course is exactly what most people are doing on the internet and likely explains the outsized amount of time that Americans are spending on mobile devices compared to personal computers.

From these figures, we can conclude that television consumption (even including streaming) has dropped off by a massive eighty-two percent over just a couple of generations, leading to a progressive decline in screen time spent consuming media as we observe younger and younger adult Americans. However, nearly everyone is equally addicted to their smart-devices at this point, spending on average over three hours per day consuming media on these handheld devices. Who can we even look to for a role model of reasonable internet and technology use? Likely not our parents (and maybe even not their parents), or perhaps even anybody that we know. No, those of us undertaking this lifestyle change will have to set our own paths.

An approach towards viewing the internet as a tool (and media consumption in general) that I've found helpful is adopting a resolution to live like it's the late 1990s and twenty-aughts again, minus the ridiculous amount of television that adults and children consumed during this time period. In my experience, this can be best implemented by engaging in two behaviors.

The first is allocating a physical desk space for a personal computer (even if it's a laptop) and viewing that as the dedicated area of your home where you sit down to accomplish specific tasks that require the use of computing technology. The goal of this approach is to view your computer as a tool, and by extension the internet as well (since these technology items are the gateway to the World Wide Web). Your home is filled with implements that carry out a particular function that you only use when needed. You don't go push random buttons on kitchen appliances for entertainment because your brain is in desperate need of stimulation; this is what a toddler might do. Ideally, you should view technology items no differently than a pen or a screwdriver — things which are otherwise inconspicuous in your home until you seek them out for a specific task.

Shifting this relationship necessitates an intentional change in one's thought patterns. Before you turn on your computer, mentally state to yourself what you are going to use it for. "I will sit down, check my email and research this product that I would like to purchase for my hobby, and then I will shut down the computer." Using it for entertainment such as playing video games is fine, as long as it's a deliberate decision along the lines of, "I am going to play this video game for one hour." The mindset of turning on these devices to click and scroll around ambiguously until you stumble upon something to entertain yourself with is what needs to go.

As both a modern white collar office worker and a writer, I understand that spending hours of your day sitting in a chair can be fatiguing, and on many occasions I have been able to squeeze out a bit more productivity from an evening by migrating to the couch with my laptop. So I hesitate to recommend an inflexibly draconian requirement of *never* moving your computer away from a physical desk, but would instead perhaps recommend that you tether yourself to that location until you judge that you were successful in shifting your viewpoint of seeing computing devices and the internet as tools.

I have witnessed and heard of too many examples of people who have developed a habit of sitting down on their couch or bed after work and wasting most of their evening away alternating between watching TV and scrolling on their smartphone, laptop, or tablet. Not only do they have to overcome the behavioral inertia of their device usage, but also the physical inertia of their comfortable position. Unless one is planning to read a book, the couch or bed for many people is likely where the untapped potential of an evening goes to die.

The second behavior that I would recommend fostering involves reducing your smartphone's presence in your life and realizing that it doesn't always have to be on hand. The idea that we always need to be connected and available to immediately respond to a call, a text message, or especially some inane notification from a social media app desperately trying to get us to open it is a farce. Most adults today recognize that modern-day digital voicemail is simply a technological transition from landline phone answering machines. Yet we seem to have forgotten as a culture that prior to widespread cellular phone adoption, people would venture out of their homes for hours and simply respond to any missed calls when they returned home. If you were expecting an urgent call you could remotely dial into your voicemail from another phone to check it, but for the most part people viewed these missed communication attempts as items which could be resolved when they were back at home.

With so much interpersonal communication today occurring on smartphones, various social contracts (often unspoken) exist in terms of our expectations of the availability of our peers, and I'd imagine the average expected response time is lower than in decades past due to the near-instant, constantly connected nature of these devices. Oftentimes these expectations seem to be inversely related to the amount of time one spends staring at their own phone screen; the heaviest addicts provide instant responses, and presuppose that others will grant them with the same, even on the most mundane of topics. A friend recently expressed his bewilderment to me that someone he knows had texted him to ask a question that was not time-sensitive, which he did not see or respond to because he was busy, and this person followed up forty-five minutes later with another message simply containing multiple question marks, implying that they felt they were overdue for a response by that point.

Performing the self-examination exercise that I laid out earlier in this chapter by looking at which apps were dominating my screen time report on my smartphone was a blunt and incontestable damnation that pretty much nothing I was doing on it was truly valuable. In a usual day, my most-used apps were the internet browser and a mobile game, each of which completely dwarfed the amount of time I spent using my phone as a communication device for calls, text messaging, and email. I found that after quitting Reddit, my other mindless scrolling and time-wasting online activities quickly fell away, and this in turn decimated the amount of time that I was spending on my smartphone. While I was certainly spending quite a bit of time on my other devices such as my computer, I was also using these devices for some productive activities; comparing the percentage of total daily time spent on each device that was meaningless or wasteful, my smartphone was unequivocally leading the pack.

This realization ended up heavily reducing the implied urgency of anything that I was doing on my phone, which further made me question why I always had it in my pocket even when I was at home. I started just leaving my smartphone on my desk next to my computer for most of the day, reasoning that the most common call or text message of potential importance (and which actually required an immediate answer) that I might receive in an average day would be work-related. To reduce the number of times per day that my phone would vibrate, I began a widespread culling of my notification settings. Some apps I only allowed to send me silent notifications, while most I restricted from ever sending me any. These days, my only audible notifications are for calls or text messages, and I feel like I'm using my phone as a tool again. Other than those core functions, about all I additionally use my phone for is keeping track of my task lists, GPS navigation, and listening to podcasts.

I'd highly recommend wholesale deleting any apps for Reddit and other social media platforms from your phone. Most are data privacy nightmares anyway, and using such apps encourages the idea that your smartphone is for entertainment. I have personally set a fifteen-minute maximum daily screen time threshold on my phone's web browser. This allows me to quickly search for information online when I'm away from my desktop computer, while avoiding the potential of frittering away my time scrolling on various mobile sites for entertainment. In fact, the browser screen time limit has completely eliminated any desire to scroll on my phone, since it encouraged me to save my daily fifteen minutes in case I actually *needed* it.

Statistically, most people have an issue with too much screen time on their mobile devices — over three hours of average daily usage just for consuming media (these figures do not include time spent actually using one's phone as a phone) across all American adults may now be the norm, but it's not normal. It's also clear that most people are increasingly using their phone as their primary gateway into the World Wide Web rather than personal computers. As such, mastering one's smartphone usage and treating it more like a landline phone that just happens to conveniently be able to be taken out of the house is a requisite step in starting to view technology as a tool again and reclaiming our lives from internet addiction. At the time I am writing this paragraph, it is 9:30 PM, and my total phone screen time today was nineteen minutes. I no longer waste two to three hours of my day on my phone.

I cannot overstate the importance of critically and honestly examining the amount of time that you are investing into various websites and apps, and whether you feel that whatever they provide to you in return is a fair value proposition. We've also covered two behaviors that I've implemented in my day-to-day life by living like it's the turn of the twenty-first century again, and how this has helped me view technology as a tool, as opposed to the widespread use of these devices as boredom-killing, magical entertainment boxes. If you are successful in this endeavor you will likely have quite a bit of additional free time on your hands, and since this is not just an exercise in reducing one's reliance on technology but also in learning to live more intentionally, we next need to ensure that this regained time is used to its maximum potential.

Chapter 20
Embrace Every Hour

The title of this chapter is a quote from one of Seneca the Younger's 124 letters on philosophical reflections addressed to his friend Lucilius, written around the year 65 AD. The first letter focuses on the value of time and opens:

> Continue to act thus, my dear Lucilius—set yourself free for your own sake; gather and save your time, which till lately has been forced from you, or filched away, or has merely slipped from your hands. Make yourself believe the truth of my words,—that certain moments are torn from us, that some are gently removed, and that others glide beyond our reach. The most disgraceful kind of loss, however, is that due to carelessness. Furthermore, if you will pay close heed to the problem, you will find that the largest portion of our life passes while we are doing ill, a goodly share while we are doing nothing, and the whole while we are doing that which is not to the purpose.[67]

Seneca acknowledges that we may lose time in our lives due to circumstances beyond our control. Where he takes issue is with people who squander those periods of time which are otherwise within their control by spending it on vapid pursuits. Interestingly, nearly two centuries earlier the satirist Roman poet Juvenal created the phrase "bread and circuses" (Latin: *panem et circenses*), observing that the Roman populace could be placated politically and their motivation dulled with the fulfillment of their base needs in the form of free grain provided by the government, plus some cheap distraction via circus games and violent gladiatorial combat. Once again, the struggles that we humans face today often have historical parallels that are stronger than one might expect; today it's massive tech companies running the circus, delivered remotely through our device screens to a similar dulling effect. For his part, Seneca defined the purpose of living as doing things that one defines as meaningful and accomplishing goals that are of importance to oneself.

If you are successful in redefining your approach towards the internet and technology in general, you will likely have a *lot* of free time on your hands to fill, even if your screen time was in line with First World averages. Using this reclaimed time wisely may possibly be the most important step in the entire process. It's about spending your time in a way that is impactful and valuable to yourself and others; building skills and setting (then achieving) progressively more difficult goals to magnify your contributions; connecting with people in a genuine manner. Fostering your own personal development, both mentally and physically, is important. As is discovering some field or topic that you have a penchant and also a passion for, a combination that could drive unique insights and lead to a contribution of real value — whether this effort is rewarded economically or not. Focused effort towards the things that you care about will do more for yourself, your family, your cause, or your community than several magnitudes more time spent posting about such things online.

I firmly believe that most people who feel unfulfilled in life are in such a state primarily because their day job feels meaningless in the grand scheme of things — an affliction that I can assure my readers they are certainly not alone in experiencing — yet they continue on that path out of pragmatism and economic self-interest as that is the application in which their labor can earn the most monetary value. The whole charade is truly quite mentally taxing, so their free time becomes recovery time to recharge for the resumption of work the next day. Spending one's time on escapist entertainment is the lowest effort way to "turn the brain off" and conserve whatever mental energy one has remaining. Unfortunately, if one's job is pointless and unfulfilling, perhaps even antagonistic to their life goals, then this free time in the evenings and weekends is the only supply of time that can potentially be harnessed as an input to building towards those dreams.

In the workplace, many younger people have shirked the nebulous bastardization of "work ethic" pushed by boomers after learning that corporate subservience is mostly an unrequited scam. But we need to keep that lesson for the workplace, and not let it spill over into our personal pursuits as well. The ideal work-life balance I think at this point is to do the bare minimum required at your job to attain and maintain a comfortable salary, and save as much of your mental energy as possible in order to dedicate as much of yourself as you can towards the things that you genuinely care about. If you are the dissatisfied employee in one of many such drab careers, you cannot go wrong simultaneously pursuing financial independence while dedicating your evening and weekends towards something that you find meaningful (which itself earns bonus points if it builds some sort of marketable skill that might allow you to assert more independence in the labor market).

Earlier when discussing behavioral inertia, I mentioned

how breaking free from it often requires a significant psychological motive to reject the status quo. Unless your life is perfectly to your expectations, and unless you are without flaw, then continuing to waste even a small part of your day scrolling on the internet and performing tasks which don't serve you should be terrifying. This realization that attaining meaning in your life, whatever you define that as, requires intentionally harnessing and directing as much of your free time towards that end as possible needs to be the foremost consideration when deciding how to spend your time.

Where to start with identifying the best places to direct one's time and efforts? I would advise beginning with the things that have always been in the back of your mind as something that you wanted to accomplish, but *thought* that you didn't have enough time for. Self-improvement is an obvious first step; you will never regret taking time to keep your body and mind sharp. Another early choice is "life skills" which I define as knowing how to do something that allows one to live more independently, commonly resulting in retaining more of one's money rather than paying someone else for their labor in that task; some skills in this category would be things like cooking, managing one's own personal finances and investments, and being able to perform basic maintenance on items you own like a car or home. The biggest decision though is what you will spend your time on in an attempt to build or contribute to something impactful to yourself and others. Everyone is different, and I can't tell you exactly what sort of legacy to spend your time in pursuit of, but I can relay my own experiences and thought process in this area.

One of the first tasks that I directed my effort towards after starting to break away from Reddit and other time-wasting websites was starting my own blog to discuss personal finance, frugality, investing, and early retirement. These are topics that

I am passionate about and in which I am constantly building up my knowledge base. In fact, much of the time that I was spending on Reddit and another dedicated investment forum was spent writing posts to exchange thoughts about these subjects and hopefully find some new sources to learn from. At a certain point I became discontented with the type of people flooding into the FIRE (Financial Independence Retire Early) community; the original basis of that movement was that *expenses* and not income were the most important variable in achieving financial independence, which fostered an inclusive spirit where people earning perfectly average middle class incomes felt like they could participate and build wealth as long as they focused on living a frugal lifestyle and investing wisely.

Many of the FIRE communities created during the aftermath of the 2008 recession have now been co-opted by tech industry yuppies from Southern California earning $300k-plus salaries who simultaneously want accolades for saving fifty percent of their income, yet are also completely tone-deaf to the fact that they're still spending double what the median American *household* earns per year. The completely-out-of-touch bubble that they dragged in with themselves drove away many longstanding members of such communities at the same time as the concept of financial independence became more popular, leading to a flood of new subscribers who caused a drastic decline in the quality of discussions. I eventually left too, and decided to start my own website to share the type of content and perspective that I wanted to see in that space. I reasoned that the amount of time and effort I was spending each day to write detailed comments on Reddit and the other forum was more than enough content to slowly fill up a website, which had the added benefits of securing ownership and financial interests over my thoughts, as well as removing myself from Reddit and the myriad of negative aspects of that platform which we have discussed at length.

In taking the leap to start up my blog and fill it with articles, I discovered the satisfaction inherent in actually *building* something. I treasured the first few comments that I received on my blog thanking me for the article or letting me know that it had been helpful more than I valued the sum total of all the comment replies that I received on Reddit over the prior decade. On Reddit I was just another generic pseudonymous Redditor, commenting on posts and links which would fall off of the front page of that community shortly after, likely never to be seen by human eyes again just a few short days later. Was that all that I wanted my legacy of contributions to the furtherance of human knowledge (and especially these topics that I cared about) to be? I realized that some of the general lack of fulfillment I was experiencing in my online time was caused by a mismatch between consumption and creation, and I would wager that this feeling applies to many young adults in today's digital world. I was spending so much time online consuming content and occasionally providing commentary, but operating within the confines of sites like Reddit, I was never able to create anything that felt like a substantially valuable contribution to a community that could stand on its own merits, either online or offline. When discussing impactful contributions to a field, people frequently reference other people, books, articles, essays, journals, podcasts, and visual media — not Redditors or Reddit posts.

Working on my blog gradually evolved into learning that I actually quite enjoyed writing, and perhaps all of those years I had spent scribing on Reddit I was simply using the site as a provisional, low-effort alternative to satiate the desire to write while at the same time opening myself to no real commitment or risk of personal criticism for my words. Building off of this, the next progressive goal in the back of my head then became the idea that I should write a book, something that I had always thought would be an interesting accomplishment but never had the dedication to get started — let alone even begin breaking down the planning process. Out of curiosity I checked the total word count across all the articles on my website, and it was about sixty thousand at the time (roughly the equivalent of a two hundred page novel), and since then I have continued to find enough worth saying to publish two or three articles per month. Clearly, if I could find that much to write about a singular topic of interest to me, then I could repeat the process with a more focused and rigorous approach. And thus the seed for what would become this book was planted.

Along similar lines I began reading actual books again; much like with writing, I had been placating a base desire to read by scrolling through online text, primarily on Reddit. I used to read quite a bit when I was younger, however reading posts and comments online had usurped this to the point where I hadn't read a single book in nearly a decade since finishing high school. I rediscovered that reading a book or detailed article was far more enjoyable than scrolling through Reddit for thirty minutes before bed. When reading for learning, in the time that it takes to read a single good book focused on a topic, you will learn much more than what can be attained from multiple times that number of hours spent browsing the corresponding Reddit community. When reading John Palmer's book *How to Brew*, I learned more from each individual chapter than I had in years of casually following discussions and reading the comments in Reddit's /r/homebrewing community. These experiences formed the basis of my Knowledge Subreddit Fallacy, when I realized that reading just one good book on a topic is enough to surpass the knowledge level of the vast majority of Redditors that hang out in that corresponding community. Reading *two* books on a particular subject, one each from influential thinkers with opposing opinions (e.g. Keynes and Hayek in economics) gives one enough mental ammunition to thoroughly wipe the floor in a debate with nearly any Redditor. That's not to say that one should invest their time in arguing online or get an overinflated ego from being more educated on a topic than a loose coalition of people who subscribed to a community primarily out of a tangential interest in it, as such behaviors are best left to be engaged in by Redditors themselves.

I had thus substituted the basic activities that I was performing on Reddit — reading and writing about topics of interest to me — for much higher-value versions of the same. Embarrassingly, it took me far too long to realize that spending time each day reading and writing with intention led to vastly more intellectual and personal development than spending my free time online while consuming various internet media sources ever had or possibly could. In the debate of contentment versus fulfillment, this is the real trap of the former I think, that it inherently biases one towards self-selecting for stagnation in all aspects of life besides those most commonly associated with hedonism, or used for projection and comparison of relative socioeconomic status. One should not be content to simply be content, but rather aspire to find fulfillment.

Besides taking up reading again, building my website, and writing this book, I have re-vectored the time each day that I used to spend on Reddit and other mindless websites into several other activities. I have maintained a dedicated exercise regimen; leveled up my cooking skills; spent more time with friends; learned about homebrewing beer and started making my own beer at home from scratch using all-grain brewing methods; bought a guitar and started practicing regularly and learning music theory. Unfortunately, that latter activity had to take a prioritization hit to give me enough time to write this book. I think that one is on the correct path towards building a fulfilling life in the modern age if they've cut their online surfing time to near-zero and redirected that time towards enriching and productive activities, but still have a backlog of items that they need to pick and choose from.

We also have to make an allowance in the day for some relaxation time. Humans only have so much endurance to expend focused mental and physical effort; the available amount likely varies per person and while I believe most of us can learn to be productive for the vast majority of a day, I don't believe that it's sustainable for someone to be grinding hard for all of their waking hours. This is just what I've found works for me: making real progress towards my goals, and only then *earning* some leisure time. At my current job, I've shifted my schedule earlier to end my day at 4:00 PM, which means that I have a solid hour or two of effort to dedicate to my personal pursuits before needing to cook or eat dinner. Diving straight into my own affairs after getting off work ensures that my time isn't stolen by behavioral inertia; I've lost too many evenings of potential in the past by claiming that I'll just relax for twenty or thirty minutes and *then* get things done, which in my experience is a promise that is rarely followed through on. Taking time to eat dinner and spend time with family while engaging in entertainment together is certainly a valuable and noble use of a portion of the evening. Following this, I find that I've recharged a bit, and have time and energy for about ninety minutes more of concentrated effort that evening.

Weekend days (or whatever days one has off from their job) are perhaps the most precious commodity of all. The entire day is yours to do with as you please, unsullied by most days' required time spent at work, including all the associated temporal costs of employment such as commuting. The weekend is not a time to lounge around in a work-induced hangover; using your time off in such a manner means that you are ceding nearly all of your waking hours to your employer, even when not at work! No, days off are *your* time to make real progress towards your personal goals, projects, and aspirations. On any day that you are not at your job, you should be able to muster at *least* the same amount of effort you would put in during a day at work towards yourself and still end up with plenty of time for relaxation. I say "at least" because chances are that your day job does not align with your passion, thus if you can spend eight hours per day working (or pretending to care about work) then as far as priorities go you should be able to find the same amount of time just two days per week to put towards things that you *actually* care about.

I have additionally met many people (most of them without children, I might add) who claim that their general life responsibilities and requisite chores built up from the week consume the majority of their weekend time. What a horribly inefficient life one must lead if such tasks as doing laundry, running to the grocery store, and cleaning the house somehow consume the majority of one's roughly thirty-two waking hours in a weekend! Of course, that is not truly the case, and such claims are simply a cover story for the reality that is more embarrassing to admit of having spent nearly the entirety of one's weekend scrolling and consuming various media.

How to structure your days off is, again, dependent on what works best for you, which is determined by a number of factors. Perhaps the largest factor is our chronotype, the behavioral manifestation of our circadian rhythm; when people talk about being an "early bird" or a "night owl" they are referring to their chronotype. I don't really fit into a neat box, and as it turns out many of us don't. I tend to lean towards morning productivity (but not *too* early) yet as I mentioned above will also frequently get some good writing time in just before bed. Sleep scientists generally agree that it's very difficult or impossible to purposely alter one's chronotype due to its genetic linkage (other than the changes which naturally occur due to age or seasonal influences), however it is possible for most of us to successfully shift our sleep and wake cycles by a couple of hours. Learn whether you have more energy in the morning or the evening, and structure your days off in such a way as to best take advantage.

In terms of actually harnessing one's energy towards more productive and fulfilling ends, there are a number of different "productivity systems" out there, but I haven't personally found any of them useful. Some people swear by the Pomodoro Technique which was invented by Francesco Cirillo during his time as a university student, named because *pomodoro* is Italian for tomato, and Cirillo used a tomato-shaped kitchen timer to break his study sessions into twenty-five-minute blocks followed by a five-minute break, with a longer twenty- to thirty-minute break awarded after iterating through the technique four times. Perhaps this method works fine for school-related tasks; personally I find it counterproductive in adult life. The twenty-five-minute work sessions are not long enough to reach a state of flow or full immersion in a task, and the five-minute breaks are too short to do anything meaningful with, indirectly encouraging silly low-commitment activities like picking up your phone and scrolling.

As I wrote in Chapter Fourteen, there is no bandage or temporary fix to finding the self-discipline and motivation to just do the things in our lives that need doing. Some of these tasks will be menial and uninteresting chores, but we should take pride in keeping our affairs in order and completing such items so that we can spend the remainder of our time doing things of higher personal value, uninhibited by thoughts of incomplete responsibilities looming over us. A "mindless" task like cleaning can be supplemented with a hands-free mental occupation such as listening to a podcast or audiobook to make more efficient and enjoyable use of one's time.

The approach that works for me is to remove most distractions and the potential for low-value time-wasting activities from my life and then to accomplish my goals based on their urgency and importance to me, while also attempting to adopt some sort of regular schedule to make my preferred behavior a habit. If I want to be a writer, then I need to write every day, which I have translated into the behavior of writing at least five hundred well-edited words per day on average (adding one hundred words to the daily goal set by Terry Pratchett when he was writing part-time). If I want to get better at brewing beer, then I need to brew regularly to build experience, which means setting aside an uninterrupted five- to six-hour block at least once per month to get a new batch in my pipeline. There is no way to circumvent the time input requirement for accomplishing any goal or building a skill, but breaking those larger tasks down into manageable daily or regularly-occurring habits is certainly an effective method. You will naturally find a balance with how many things you can sustainably work towards at once in your available free time, and may then have to pick and choose which to devote your full attention to for the foreseeable future.

If I am doing a thought-intensive process like writing on a weekend, I'll write for three or so hours in the morning, as I find that to be about my limit for complete concentration on a demanding mental engagement. I will then switch to another task for a while that gives my mind a break like exercising, making lunch, or cleaning, after which I will resume writing for a while or taking care of any other tasks that require mental focus. Interweaving these mindless tasks that still ultimately need to get done allow me a much-needed temporary break from focused mental effort, while still maintaining a complete stretch of productivity for my whole morning and early afternoon. I am not a stereotypical "morning person" but I do enjoy the feeling of having a solid day's worth of accomplishments under my belt by mid-afternoon, so I will often fight against my inclination to sleep in and instead just get up and get started on my day at 6:30 or 7:00 AM on my days off. This leaves my weekend evenings open for socializing and relaxation — leisure time is certainly more delightful when it is earned following a fulfilling day, as opposed to when one's weekends are filled with nothing but lounging around.

When you do indulge in entertainment, make sure that it is high quality. I've presented my case that Reddit and other forms of social media or online content served on an infinite scroll have some of the lowest value propositions across the board. Much of the content presented as entertaining on these sites is not actually funny or interesting, they are poor proxies for maintaining social relationships, and for educational purposes the depth of knowledge of the users as reflected in the content they produce is near the bottom of the barrel. Essentially, everything that you can do on these sites has a far superior alternative activity.

As already suggested, you can read a book instead of reading stories and comments on social media. Rather than spending several hours each day scrolling through video and image posts, go watch thirty minutes or an hour of a television series that you find enjoyable, or sit down to watch a movie once in a while. Video games are fine as long as they do not take over your life; I'd avoid online gaming entirely with the only exception being if you're playing together with real-world friends. A decent single player video game could certainly be more engaging and immersive to some people than television or movies, while generally having an end and not being able to infinitely suck your time away like the complete addictive monstrosity (rivaling social media) that competitive online gaming has evolved into. Spend more time socializing in person. Play some board games with your family and friends rather than gathering around a screen.

There's nearly an endless amount of worthier manners — more productive or more enjoyable — in which one can spend their time instead of scrolling on Reddit or any other time-wasting website. Only you can ultimately decide which things constitute meaningful ways to spend your time, or what goals to pursue that feel important and assist in building towards your ideal life. Criticism of how you spend your time should either be ignored completely (in the case that it contradicts what you truly feel to be correct), or should be weighed against any net positive impact of your actions on yourself and others. Oftentimes, the reward of time well-spent is simply a sense of personal accomplishment or fulfillment. Whether we have succeeded in any endeavor or spent our time wisely, is not for fame or wealth to determine, but only how well we measure up to our own expectations.

Chapter 21
Thirty Days to Fix Your Brain

I firmly believe that constant interconnectedness and the prevalence of digital addiction in modern society is having negative mental effects on all of us. Most of the scientific research on social media up to this point has been focused on adolescents, likely due to a number of factors such as a societal impulse to protect children from harm, the increased vulnerability of their developing brains, and rapidly rising rates of depression and anxiety observed among teenagers in the US and UK since 2012 (for which recent studies are demonstrating a causal relationship with social media).[68] What of adults, though, especially as the ranks of adulthood is beginning to be filled with those who have no memories of growing up in a world without the internet in everyone's pocket? As noted earlier, some Redditors still refuse to admit that Reddit is even a social media site at all, and yet more concede that it is, but maintain the probable misconception that it's not as bad for its users as other social media platforms.

Marine biologist Daniel Pauly coined a term called "shifting baseline syndrome" in 1995 to describe how scientists tended to use the state of fisheries at the start of their careers as the baseline against which to judge population decline, rather than comparing to the population levels prior to human fishing activity. As each successive generation redefined their perceived baseline, the true scale of change was further lost and obscured. Additional research into Pauly's theory expanded it to other areas of ecology such as environmental degradation and proposed two underlying causes behind shifting baselines: the aforementioned information loss between generations, and "personal amnesia" where individuals forget their own experiences over time, mentally updating their past perceptions to reflect their current observations.[69] This is likely due to the cognitive effect of recency bias where people tend to overweight the significance of recent events compared to their older experiences.

It doesn't take a wild extrapolation to postulate that the shifting baseline syndrome likely applies to areas beyond ecology, including cognitive psychology — our internal mental processes. One's mental state is a firsthand experience which can't be transmitted exactly between people or across generations. If technology addiction continues to be as widespread as it is today, it will be so normalized to future researchers that it will become their baseline against which to measure the impact of whatever new technology developments arise. In the future, it will be difficult for researchers to accurately assess any *cumulative* negative mental effects of social media and technology overuse beginning from the pre-smartphone era, even if they had access to the most fastidious personal diaries from that time.

Even those people alive today with memories prior to widespread societal digital addictions likely don't remember exactly how they felt in those times. If they do believe that life was better back then, it may simply be the effect of rose-tinted glasses or exuberance born of childhood innocence. It's very likely that you can pinpoint a difference in how you cognitively feel between today and yesterday; maybe even a week ago. But several years ago? Unless your life underwent a seismic, defining shift during that period, your brain will fall back on your recent perceptions to fill in that information. A general default of the human psyche is that our memory is rarely as reliable as we'd like to believe.

As such, most people are likely to say how they've generally felt recently is where their mental baseline is. Short-term deviations such as illness will be easily noted from that shifted baseline. But if a long-term slow degradation in our mental state occurred over many years due to increased use of social media and wasteful web scrolling, how would we even notice when our brain's functions can muddle our own memories?

The most commonly claimed negative effect of digital addiction is brain fog. While it's not a medical diagnosis or a clinical term, brain fog describes a subjective feeling of cognitive impairment — that one does not have full mental clarity. Often people describe this manifesting as a difficulty in focusing, frequent forgetfulness, or a feeling that thinking through or solving complex problems (even when similar ones have been successfully tackled in the past) is just out of reach. Neuroscientist Manfred Spitzer calls this specific cognitive impairment "digital dementia," proposing that an overuse of digital technology causes short-term memory pathways to atrophy from reduced utilization.

The simplest way to find an answer as to whether digital dementia truly exists is to run our own self-experiments. If we stop using technology for entertainment, and cease falling back on it as a primary reflex when solving problems, can we experience a positive cognitive change which can likely be attributed to that decision? You can sit around waiting for psychologists to publish some comprehensive paper on the cumulative negative effects of digital addiction, or you can begin making your own observations about a lived experience right now.

To that end, I propose the following: for the next full month, completely avoid using Reddit and instead invest whatever amount of time per day you would spend on the site into any activity that you deem productive or enriching. That's it. You don't even have to repurpose that time into an offline activity, for example if you have a goal to start a website or begin learning computer programming, technology is a necessary tool to employ in those pursuits. The most important aspect is that you completely stay off of Reddit, and that you do not allow the time you've gained to be absorbed into other time-wasting activities.

This is a concept heavily inspired by the "digital detox" proposed by Cal Newport in *Digital Minimalism*. He advises taking a thirty-day break from all "optional technologies," using this time to explore satisfying and meaningful activities, and then after the thirty days slowly reintroducing only those technologies that we can articulate the value of. Detoxification in this instance refers to the process of returning one's body to homeostasis after long-term use of an addictive substance; using the term in conjunction with social media or technology tacitly states that one believes the growing body of evidence indicating that the responses they elicit from the brain's reward circuitry warrant classifying them as an addictive drug-adjacent activity.

As someone whose life was consumed by wasting time on technology, I found Newport's all-in approach overwhelming and quickly failed, multiple times. He suggests several explanations for why a "nontrivial number of people" participating in his experiment failed to complete the thirty-day digital detox; these reasons are valid contributors but I don't believe they tell the whole story. Instead, I wondered if Newport — who admits to never having a social media

account, or ever spending much time surfing the web —
simply lacked the personal experience with digital addiction to
understand the siren song of these platforms, as well as the
sheer amount of time that he was asking some of his readers
to figure out how to fill overnight.

What I am instead proposing is a *gradual* digital detox,
starting with Reddit (or really whichever single technology
habit you find the most time-consuming). Quitting everything
at once is surprisingly difficult for most people. You can keep
whatever time you were spending on other social media apps,
video games, chat rooms, and video streaming. The only rule
with this is that you must accomplish whichever new activity
that you deem productive or meaningful first, and you must
do it for at least as long as the average amount of time you
would have spent on Reddit or whichever service you are
quitting. This guarantees that your other technology habits
cannot expand to fill the gap you've created, because you got
your productive activity done before engaging with any of
them.

The primary goal with this approach is to re-acquaint you
with the sense of accomplishment from applying your time in
a meaningful manner, to explore new hobbies and gain
inspiration, while avoiding the inevitable (if scrolling and
consuming media was your primary evening activity) crushing
defeat of quitting every non-essential technology cold turkey.
In my experience, that sense of true accomplishment from
creating tangible things in the "real world" was the most
powerful force motivating me to continue reducing my
wasteful web browsing even further. I would often find myself
continuing with my productive activities long past the
minimum time that I had mandated for them.

If you are successful, you can iteratively apply this process
going forward, cutting out one undesirable activity at a time.
It's certainly also possible to incrementally reduce the amount

of time you are spending on several websites or apps, but I personally found that declaring I was unequivocally quitting yet another service in totality was far more impactful and motivating. There's no requirement that you need to wait until the end of a month before cutting out another platform or activity — as in Newport's digital detox, the purpose of this time is that you must spend at least that long away from each service before deciding if you are going to add it back into your life and if so, how much of it. For example, if you quit Reddit two weeks ago and it has been a rousing success, you may also decide to quit Discord at this time, however you still must see out the remainder of your month away from Reddit and a further month going forward with no Discord use. If you have more than a few time-wasting technology platforms that you frequent, it may be helpful to write down these commitment dates.

Using this gradual digital detox technique, I slowly quit Reddit and all other social media sites, stopped browsing several internet forums, and quit massively multiplayer online video games. I personally found the one-at-a-time approach to reforming my technology habits far more manageable than attempting to quit everything at once (which I had failed half a dozen or more times, quickly falling back into my old usage patterns). Because I failed the complete digital detox within a few days to a couple of weeks every time, I was never able to get past the time threshold required to experience most of the positive mental effects of reduced technology use, or to break that psychological compulsion to return to these activities.

The gradual digital detox is what allowed me to finally get past that barrier. After spending close to a month away from Reddit and replacing that time in my day with more constructive activities, I had no desire to return to participate on the site in any capacity. It was not like a switch was instantaneously flipped, but more of a slow decay; I went from attempting to habitually navigate to Reddit probably twenty times on day one, to realizing I hadn't thought about Reddit or tried to access the site all day near the end of the month. My speculation is that this is a type of withdrawal process from digital addiction, and that the common wisdom that it takes four weeks or a month to change a habit is nearly exactly on the money.

An anecdotal report of my own experience in breaking away from Reddit is that the brain fog that I was experiencing on a near-daily basis went away. I changed nothing about my lifestyle, diet, or any aspect of my life other than cutting out most of the time I was spending scrolling online on my computer and my phone by not going on Reddit, and instead substituting that time for more meaningful activities such as reading books. A couple of weeks later it was as if a mental cloud had slowly begun to lift and revealed occasional glimpses of the mental clarity that I knew I had experienced in the past, but in recent years had felt beyond my grasp. My attention span began to recover, and I rediscovered an ability to reach a state of flow when engaged in tasks of interest to me, no longer feeling as if I had to check my phone or open a browser tab to impulsively check some time-wasting website like Reddit multiple times per hour.

Additionally, my general day-to-day mood and outlook on life improved. I previously had a vague idea that Reddit was a gathering place for those looking to vent negative emotions; nearly every day that I commented on the site, I would get some percentage of replies that were rude and condescending or engaged in personal attacks, even when posting about relatively inane topics. I hadn't yet fully realized that even if I avoided engaging with these Redditors, their unique brand of toxic misanthropy was still able to affect my mentality as if it were some sort of miasma hanging over the site. I'm not alone in that feeling, for example, one user posted in /r/NoSurf about how they were motivated to take a thirty-day break from Reddit "because it's extremely negative and the users here are extremely nihilistic and hostile." Very few people seem to have *ever* issued praise of Redditors in general — the most common descriptors that are used in relation to them are negative traits typically associated with low emotional intelligence. It's a self-feeding, cynical environment that conditions one to always assume the worst in other people. I can't fully explain why I had a high tolerance for continuously reading comments from such people when if I was interacting with a real-life person who conversed in the manner stereotypical of power Redditors, I would seek to exit that conversation as quickly as possible and avoid further contact with that individual.

Some portion of the above positive mood changes could also be explained by cutting myself off from the majority of news updates when I quit Reddit. Studies have shown what most of us have suspected for quite some time, that consuming negative news can lead to increased feelings of distress, anxiety, fear, sadness, and anger.[70] Humans have an evolutionary tendency to desire being able to predict and stay informed of potential danger, which would have increased our chances to survive in an uncertain, risky world. If you feel that the news these days consists mostly of "bad news" it's because that's what sells well to our primal instincts. Analysis of the tone of COVID-19-related news led by Bruce Sacerdote at Dartmouth College using a language-classification technique found that eighty-seven percent of stories by major US media outlets were negative in tone, versus fifty percent for non-US major media sources and sixty-four percent for scientific journals.[71] Expanding beyond the coronavirus topic which had the most negative news coverage relative to other topics, the researchers report that "the most popular stories in *The New York Times*, *CNN*, and the *BBC* have high levels of negativity for all types of articles." Disconnecting from the news, especially from American media outlets, is clearly a compelling method of removing unnecessary negativity from one's life.

I addressed in Chapters Twelve and Thirteen how quitting Reddit and other time-wasting websites led to periods of solitude returning in my life, and the underrated aspect of having time to allow one's mind to wander and thus arrive at one's own conclusions, rather than constantly absorbing the thoughts of others online. Today, many people describe the state in which some type of media is not being pumped into their mind as "boredom." For those unplugging from the internet and reclaiming their life in the real world, these periods of time offer a valuable opportunity to rediscover one's own inner voice, develop independently as a person, and spark creativity. I seized these opportunities to intentionally plan my next activity, rather than habitually turning to my former energy and dopamine traps. If one is truly bored, it does not take much self-awareness to articulate the reason why they may be feeling that way, or what a meaningful use of one's time might be rather than turning to some low-quality distraction as a bandage fix.

Modifying Cal Newport's approach into a thirty-day *gradual* digital detox is something that I found to be a wonderfully effective method of reclaiming my life from wasting time on technology. The iterative method of quitting one digital habit at a time broke the process up into manageable steps, helped me get reacquainted with learning how to spend my time in the analog world, and avoided the crushing failure and relapse which can manifest from trying to completely upend and reform one's entire life overnight. Give it a try, starting with whichever website or app that you waste the most time per day on. Then redirect that time into any tasks that have been on your back burner, usurped by your online habits; something that you believe to be productive and will reward you with a sense of accomplishment. You just may discover a positive change, find the best aspects of yourself, and gain the motivation to reorient your life in the real world.

Chapter 22
Maintaining Practical Uses of Reddit

Something that I have not yet addressed in these pages is whether Reddit can be used to some extent as a tool, and though that value seems to be steadily declining (at the same time as the site becomes more addictive, increasing the risk of getting sucked into scrolling) it is certainly worth an exploration. My goal is to encourage people to stop using Reddit for entertainment, and to discredit it as an authoritative source of information. However, it still retains some value as a crowdsourcing tool for opinions, troubleshooting, and basic information, provided that one approaches what they read there with a healthy dose of skepticism and critically vets information with other sources.

For example, Reddit has the potential to be a good source of user reviews and testimonials for a product or service, as long as a user is aware of the astroturfing and guerilla advertising which seem to have only grown more widespread on the site over time. Prior to trusting any opinions about products or services, a user should foster an attitude of investigating the likelihood that a post came from a genuine person or whether an account seems to be oddly exuberant in their promotion of it, or even more obviously has an established history of doing so. I frequently seek out negative reviews on Reddit of brands and products that I am considering purchasing, more so to see if there is a reason *not* to buy something rather than to be convinced of its merits. It would take much more effort for an astroturfer to disparage the products of all of their competitors as opposed to boosting their own.

Reddit can also be a resource for problem-solving and troubleshooting technical issues. You may be able to find a previous thread where a user posted the same issue and another user helped solve it. Or if the issue is unique, you can create a new thread and if you are lucky, someone who is knowledgeable will come along and lend their time to help you out (though this is certainly not the expected outcome). I have found many solutions on Reddit for problems with things such as computer software, hardware, and car maintenance that I was unable to solve on my own (or with other online sources).

Finally, I believe that Reddit can be a great place to locate basic, beginner-level information for hobbies. This often lies not in interactions with other users, but in the collection of resources that some subreddit moderators assemble for their community. On desktop computers this information can be found in the sidebar to the right of the page, and on mobile views users can navigate to the context menu and click the "community information" link. If one is getting started with a new hobby, it is at least worth checking out whether the associated subreddit has created some sort of "getting started" or "frequently asked questions" page. However, as I cautioned in Chapter Seven, one must be very careful to avoid the pitfall of thinking that these communities have much educational value beyond the novice level.

Web surfers clearly see the value of Reddit as a tool for

crowdsourced information, as a Google Trends analysis of search terms shows that queries involving the phrase "Reddit" are continuing to grow over time, while queries involving most other active social media platforms peaked years ago. The thing is, Reddit's search feature built into their site is absolutely abhorrent, and Google is much better at indexing and serving Reddit's own pages to match a particular query. Therefore, when one wants to search Reddit for particular information, they are better served doing so by proxy via Google or some other search engine.

Another factor in the rise of Reddit as a search engine augmentation phrase is that "Google Search Is Dying," according to the title of a February 2022 post by software engineer Dmitri Brereton on his personal blog. Brereton claims that the results that Google produces for a particular query are deteriorating in quality due to a multitude of reasons, one of which is Search Engine Optimization (SEO).[72] SEO is essentially the process of figuring out how to game Google's algorithm to obtain a higher position in the search results and thus get more web traffic. Over the past couple of decades, SEO has gone from being mainly a tool used by bloggers desiring a bit more visibility for their genuine content to something abused by the designers of bots harnessing artificial intelligence to algorithmically generate content — primarily to appeal to the Google algorithm, not to humans — with the sole goal of getting a click on their site filled with a minefield of advertisements. You've almost certainly happened upon one of these sites at some point; they're most frequently a massive wall of text stuffed full of keywords, phrases, and queries a user might input into an internet search engine; often the grammar is poor, the writing has no flow or is downright nonsensical (in the unique manner that only a low-quality Natural Language Processing bot can produce), and the answer or information that you clicked on the site for is commonly incorrect.

I can confirm Brereton's reasoning. For over a decade before he wrote his post, I have been appending "Reddit" or "forum" to search engine queries which did not produce any useful results in a bid to narrow the results down to a relevant discussion between actual humans. Lately I have been doing so with increasing frequency as the search engine's own ads, algorithmically-generated clickbait, and overly long, tangential video links dominate search engine results.

My method to access information on Reddit from search engines without getting sucked into browsing the site is via cached pages. Several popular search engines take occasional snapshots of web pages as a backup in case the current page is unavailable. Since the cached page is served from the search engine's own domain, if one has a site blocker blacklisting Reddit's domain, the cached page will still load. However, clicking any links on the cached page will redirect to the live Reddit domain and will then be blocked. Using this method, one is able to only view the specific page from their search which potentially contains the information that they seek without risking falling into a rabbit hole browsing elsewhere on Reddit. If there is no cached page available, I simply move on and look for the information elsewhere, as I am unwilling to disable my site blockers.

It is my experience that old-school internet forums dedicated to a particular topic are nearly always a superior source of information compared to Reddit. I believe this is because experts congregate there in higher concentrations — only someone who is truly passionate about a hobby or topic would sign up to a forum centered on that singular subject — whereas Reddit users can participate in any community on the site with no extra steps, incentivizing users to subscribe to dozens of communities they *might* have an interest in.

The rise of Reddit as a massive discussion aggregator has

led to a general decline in the number of independent internet forums, however most popular hobbies or interests seem to have at least one active forum left. I am not suggesting by any means that you dive headfirst into participating in these sites as an alternative to Reddit, but perhaps simply checking them before Reddit when searching for information on the web. Despite oftentimes hosting more experts than Reddit does, it should not be assumed that the average poster on these forums has much of a clue what they are talking about, or that a user's post count is correlated with their knowledge level. Unless the forum is heavily moderated, it is not uncommon to see the same type of negative behaviors characteristic of terminally online users of other internet spaces.

I no longer contribute any content or discussion to Reddit or any other forums despite occasionally using these sites as a resource as described above, and I would encourage others to do the same. Therefore, what I am proposing actively encourages a tragedy of the commons, at least as it relates to online social websites. Clearly, if everybody followed this approach of selfishly taking what information they find valuable and never contributing, Reddit and similar platforms would be utterly empty and cease to exist. In a real-world community, such a selfish approach would warrant a scornful backlash from the other members of the community. But because these social media platforms have stripped human interaction down to such a rudimentary level, consequently what springs forth from them are also pale imitations of community. You owe nothing to this crude substitute of the human experience that we have been provided by the likes of Reddit.

Let the people who have not yet come to this realization continue contributing their labor for free to entities like Reddit and consuming the low-quality content produced therein. If, like me, you have an idealistic view of the internet as a place for knowledge sharing and exchange, you will only drive yourself to frustration trying to get Reddit and online forums to fit that mold. There are better, more impactful — either for yourself, or your real-world community — ways to spend your time.

This is not a contradiction with the prior chapter; I love online content and think the internet is an amazing tool for free learning. I absolutely encourage passionate people to create content to share on the web, but in a decentralized manner where they own what they produce and have the potential of seeing financial benefit to themselves rather than handing everything over to some monolithic social media giant like Reddit.

One final potential practical use of Reddit that I think is worth touching on is using the site for advertising one's products, business, or online content. On the one hand, it would be fairly hypocritical of me to complain that astroturfing is a factor contributing to Reddit going downhill but then to recommend others to engage in that behavior for their own personal gain. On the other hand, some individuals advertising their small business on the site (if done legally) will hardly be the straw that breaks the camel's back and is far from the most nefarious activity that occurs on the site.

Reddit is incredibly disconnected from the ideal of what an online social platform should be and increasingly appears to be shifting towards being a net-negative for society; there is nearly nothing about the site worth preserving and conversely there is little of value to feel bad about corrupting. I cannot blame a disillusioned Redditor for exploiting the site to their own benefit, especially if the content that they are submitting can reasonably be presented as equal or higher quality than the normal fare found in a particular community.

A final word of caution: use these practical applications of Reddit sparingly and as a single tool in your toolbox. You should rely on a variety of sources of information. As I advised in Chapter Twelve, cultivate a habit of thinking through things for yourself and attempting a fair shake at solving problems on your own, rather than just running to your preferred internet search engine of choice to be spoon-fed an answer when you are curious about something.

Chapter 23

How You Can Help Fix the Internet

As my readers can no doubt infer by this point, I view the majority of the total minutes that world citizens are spending online as wasteful — and I don't mean wasteful in the sense of not being used to add to some country's standard economic measures of productivity. Rather, that the users themselves for the most part recognize the time they're spending scrolling as worthless but continue to do it anyway due to some combination of subversive psychological manipulation engaged in by these platforms, plus a lack of personal motivation and discipline to articulate and execute an alternative use of their time. Excluding search engines, the top twenty websites that the world is spending the most time on are dominated by video streaming sites and social media platforms.[73] Unprecedented levels of media consolidation (both online and offline) have created a winner-takes-all system in the competition for our attention on the internet. The number one website by total time spent annually across all global users was Google, with over 210 billion hours. Number two? YouTube (also owned by Google) with over 140 billion hours. Reddit holds slot fifteen with 3.1 billion hours, less than one percent of the total time-on-page garnered by top dog Google's associated projects.

The World Wide Web was originally invented by British scientist Tim Berners-Lee in 1989 while he was working at CERN, and was conceived as a method of more quickly enabling the sharing of information between scientists across the globe. The CERN design documentation states, "At its heart, WorldWideWeb is a word processor ...but with links." The Internet (of which the World Wide Web is just one service but often colloquially referred to as the former) had its technological foundation as a wide-area computer communications network beginning in the late 1960s with the ARPANET (Advanced Research Projects Agency Network), also created primarily for academic use and information-sharing between researchers at various universities working mostly on military research projects sponsored by the US government.

In a 2017 interview with NPR's *All Tech Considered* blog, Berners-Lee said about the Web, "The idea was that it could put anything on it. I never imagined that it would kind of have everything on it."[74] So it goes with inventions and new technology, that they often evolve and are iterated upon in ways that the initial designer could not have foreseen. Lou Montulli, the inventor of web browser cookies back in 1994, also has some misgivings about the state of his creation. Cookies were created by Montulli to allow websites to remember information about a user (enabling them to do things like build and retain a shopping cart on a retail website), and he did not predict the monstrosity of advertisement-related tracking that they would enable today. In an episode of NPR's *Planet Money* podcast, Montulli said, "No matter your best intentions, technology, once released into the wild, will be used however people choose to use it.

You're going to build something, and then, it will evolve over time, and you will have no control over it. And at a certain point, you just have to deal with it."[75]

So this is the web that we have to deal with today, but is it the web we're stuck with forever? That depends on how many people care enough to fight for change. I would estimate that the odds of societal pressure forcing this issue any time soon are not high — most people that I know do not care one single lick about trackers, data privacy, or the internet continuing to become less decentralized. I'm mostly met with looks of bewilderment when I mention that I am no longer willing to wantonly create accounts for "free" services that collect (and possibly sell) my personal information and device telemetry. There seem to be several groups of people apathetic to action on this topic: those who don't fully understand the scale at which this is occurring and have not yet formed an opinion either way; lazy defeatists who recognize the issue but claim it's too widespread to do anything about; and finally subscribers to the heavily flawed "I have nothing to hide" argument. Perhaps people need to be personally affected in a negative manner before they will be compelled to action.

I can't say for sure when the internet began to *feel* different. Maybe it was just the hopeful promise of a new technology wearing off. Maybe it's me growing older. All I know is that in my opinion, the internet wasn't supposed to be a place where a handful of techno-conglomerates control (even indirectly) everything that you can see and say. Eventually, I established a habit of deleting and making a new Reddit account every so often to avoid too much information about myself being aggregated in one place. I recall one instance around 2019 when I went to create a new account, and after posting for a couple of days realized that nobody was voting on or replying to my comments. I checked the profile for the account that I had made from a private browser window, and sure enough, the account appeared to not exist — I was shadowbanned. According to a Reddit administrator, "A shadowban is the tool we currently use to ban people when they are caught breaking a rule. It causes their submitted content and user profile page to be visible only to themselves while logged in."

The issue with this explanation is that I hadn't broken any site rules that I was aware of. I messaged Reddit's administrators about my issue and never received a response. When I began researching and reading about others who were also shadowbanned on a new account for no obvious reason, I discovered that a common thread was that the users signed up while using a Virtual Private Network (VPN) connection or the Tor privacy network, and the consensus was that they suspected Reddit had lazily correlated using an IP address associated with many VPNs with being a spambot or a ban evader, instantly and automatically shadowbanning such accounts. This memory stands out to me because it marked the first time that I had to actually make a binary choice between privacy or not being able to use an online service. Sure enough, I disabled my VPN connection then made another Reddit account and all was functioning properly. In exchange, Reddit got to see my real IP address. Should I have had to make that decision? Not on the World Wide Web that Tim Berners-Lee originally envisioned. Will scenarios like this become more common as time goes on, and these massive techno-conglomerates become more bold in their data collection and exploitation processes? That those who want to opt out on the principle of privacy simply will be told that they're not welcome as users of online platforms?

You can't fix the internet by participating within the box that has been created by media consolidation, corporate buyouts, and the rise of winner-takes-all technology platforms. Even if you relentlessly block all advertisements, you're still giving these sites something of value. This is either in the form of your personal data (in many cases, even users with VPNs have a unique web browser fingerprint which can be used to identify them unless they've taken specific steps to block browser fingerprinting such as using Tor or Brave Browser), or by making contributions to the site and creating posts or comments for other users to consume, thus causing users who don't block ads to spend more time scrolling on the site and indirectly leading to revenue generation. Recall the 90–9–1 principle: only about ten percent of users are creating or contributing to content on a site, therefore "lurkers" must generate the majority of page views (and it follows, advertisement revenue). Additionally, many of these platforms are allowed to skate by on venture capital funding when they would have otherwise failed in a capitalist market, because as the story goes, they'll capture the majority of the market share at any cost and *then* make money for their investors once they achieve economies of scale. Blocking ads yet continuing to actively use these sites is often not hurting them as much as one may initially suspect.

There's a common expression among capital market participants to "vote with your wallet." It's referring to the fact that people should purchase products that reflect their personal values. But what gets lost with that saying is that what you *don't* buy can be more important than what you do buy. For example, if you don't like the concept of disposable dinnerware because you're concerned about waste but purchase it anyway, you're effectively sending a signal to the manufacturer to produce more of that product. If enough consumers collectively stopped purchasing paper and plastic plates, manufacturers would stop making them. Where the concept of voting with your wallet breaks is in the free-to-play (F2P) model; people may think they're winning (or at least not losing) because they get to use the platform for free or play the video game for free. F2P online video games with microtransactions rake in most of their money from "whales," the singular person per thousand or ten thousand players who spend a ridiculous amount of money on the game. Often the players who play for free or spend very little detest this model altogether compared to the days of spending a flat sixty dollars for a complete video game, yet don't realize that they're furthering the system even by playing for free. If the majority of players quit every game operating on F2P models, they would quickly die off and developers would be forced to move back to the old model. Therefore, I'm proposing a modified idiom for the free-to-play world: "vote with your attention."

Voting with your attention accounts for the fact that in the modern service economy, money is not always required to be extracted from us in order to "create value" for another party. It's an admittance that most of us share some of the blame for the state of the internet today, besides perhaps that small contingent of techies who operate on diehard Free and Open-Source Software (FOSS) principles and utterly refuse to use anything else — they were probably right all along, even if some of them were pretty smug about the whole thing. For the internet to live up to its potential, we need to move outside of the walled garden set up by these techno-conglomerates and recreate a democratic internet. The system that will best serve us is not the one that has been determined by a half-dozen companies, convenient though it may be.

When voting with our attention, we only use the services that reflect our personal values. One who complains about a service making user-unfriendly changes or objects to actions taken by its parent corporation yet continues to use it regularly is little different from its most passionate fans. Daily and monthly active users are some of the most important metrics to these platforms right now, and chances are that counting as one of these users (especially if you're not using an ad blocker) is one of the most impactful things that you do when spending time online. Instead, we need to use the websites and platforms that reflect the internet we want to see. For me this means primarily consuming content from independent sources, that is, those owned and operated by individuals or non-profits as opposed to governments or corporations.

In fact, maybe we should all contribute to such a World Wide Web ourselves. I believe that many of the biggest issues facing the internet could be solved if most people simply had their own website. A platform that they definitively control, where they can post whatever they want without worrying about changing terms of service encroaching on that ability, or relying on any sort of magnanimity by the techno-conglomerates. A domain name and web hosting for a basic site running the open-source WordPress software (which requires no coding knowledge) can be had for just a few dollars per month — which at least in my opinion, even if one's website never earns a dime, is a worthwhile cost for fostering online independence. You can even have multiple websites, for example I own the commercial domain for my own name, www.jacobdesforges.com, and I also have my financial blog which I keep private and write under a pseudonym to allow me to freely post about my personal finances without directly making such sensitive information about me available to anybody who types my name into a search engine.

Anything that one would feel urged to post about on various platforms online could just be put on their own site instead. Post photographs for your friends and family to view on your own domain rather than on social media. For job seeking, host your resume and a portfolio of work on your site versus wasting time with LinkedIn or whichever mostly useless "professional social networking" platform supersedes it in the future. Instead of posting knowledge contributions and helpful guides to Reddit or forums related to your hobbies and interests, write them on your own domain where you will fully own the content and decide if anybody gets to make money off of serving advertisements alongside it. If your content is high quality, it may rank well in search engines for others to discover organically. Additionally, operating one's own website encourages a habit of mainly investing time in creating effortful content rather than perpetuating the delusion that anybody cares about the sound bites of your political opinions, what your meal at a restaurant looked like, or other daily inanities that people fill their social media feeds with.

I can imagine a common objection is that social media has updates from all of one's friends and family in a few places, and that visiting dozens of personal sites to check in on peoples' lives and projects would be cumbersome and time-consuming. That would be true if one was archaically navigating to dozens of sites manually on a regular basis and visually looking for updates since their last visit. However, this is a problem that was solved a long time ago (in 1999!) with Really Simple Syndication (RSS). It's a computer-readable web feed that provides updates from a website in a standardized format, for example when a blog author employing an RSS feed publishes a new post it would also create a new entry in their RSS feed. End users typically employ an RSS reader to aggregate and monitor a list of feeds from various websites that they would like to subscribe to. RSS saves quite a bit of time on behalf of the user by eliminating manual website checking while ensuring that they never miss an update from the sites and authors that they like to follow.

In a way, RSS is a kind of spiritual precursor to content aggregator sites like Reddit. The late Aaron Swartz (a developer and part-owner of Reddit during it's earliest days) contributed to the development of RSS prior to his work at Reddit by co-authoring the RSS 1.0 specification. As I mentioned in the previous chapter, the rise of Reddit as an all-in-one site hosting discussions on any topic under the sun led to a general decline in the number of internet forums that exist. However, I believe that Reddit also played a role in declining interest in RSS. A Google Trends analysis for "RSS" shows that search phrase peaking in popularity in December 2005, six months after Reddit was founded. Since then, searches of the phrase "RSS" have declined to just five percent of that peak value today in 2023. The term "RSS reader" shows a nearly identical graph, while searches for the term "RSS how to" hit an all-time-high in 2009 and today stand at about twenty percent of that former peak popularity.

Amusingly, many non-technical people today are using RSS in their daily lives and don't even know about it; anybody who listens to podcasts is reliant on RSS as it is the backbone technology used to update podcast directories, allowing their podcast player to know when the latest episode of their favorite shows is ready to be downloaded. A market outlook conducted by *Statista* identified 88.9 million podcast listeners in the United States in 2022 (nearly double the number of listeners compared to 2017) and projects this audience to continue growing at a decent rate at least into the near future.[76] So even if interest in RSS is declining, it's unlikely to die as a technology anytime soon as some people have claimed; that little orange button with the white radio icon will probably persist for quite some time.

There's even a movement for re-popularizing RSS for article and content delivery among web users. A 2018 *Wired* article by Brian Barrett titled "It's Time for an RSS Revival" presents the older technology as a preferable alternative to today's deluge of algorithmically-determined content and argues that RSS readers should make a comeback based on their merits. Barrett writes that "the lasting appeal of RSS remains the parts that haven't changed: the unfiltered view of the open web, and the chance to make your own decisions about what you find there."[77]

One thing that I personally like about RSS is it feels like using a more manageable, less overwhelming version of the internet. There is no fear of missing out when every update that you might care about is delivered into a queue to be accessed whenever you have the time, compared to other social media sites with a feed of constantly changing user-submitted content. With no need to manually check websites for updates, I found that shifting to an RSS reader disincentivized the behavior of habitually opening a new browser tab and navigating to a favorite website for amusement or procrastination (even further than the employment of my site blocker already had). My RSS reader's feed was now akin to my podcasting app — something that I checked only when I had time to specifically engage in that form of media consumption, rather than being the default entertainment pastime that many people use the internet as today.

Curating media consumption to only high quality, insightful sources likewise applies to RSS feeds — I absolutely am not recommending using this tool to recreate a Reddit-esque infinite feed of articles on topics of tangential interest to you. An RSS reader should ultimately cause you to spend *less* time staring at your devices than you were previously. So don't randomly browse around to find sites to fill your RSS feed with for the sake of loading it with content. Organic discovery involves a process more akin to: *while seeking knowledge on a search engine, one of the sites that I was led to had particularly insightful or interesting (but practically useful) content in the linked article, and upon investigating other posts on that site I found many of the author's writings also fit that standard. I would like to read more from this site in the future as I expect it to be relevant or useful to me, therefore I will add it to my RSS feed.* The recommendation approach is also a fair methodology to discovering content, where one has heard good things about a website from another source that they hold in high esteem and finds that the content satisfies the thresholds for quality and usefulness that they've set for inclusion into the list of sites that they subscribe to. Most of the books in my reading list, for example, landed there because I saw an interesting quotation or reference to them in whichever book that I'm currently reading, and noted them down to check out later.

It is even still possible to subscribe to a YouTube channel via RSS, although Google has made the process less transparent over the years, likely in a bid to get people to use YouTube's native subscription feature, thus getting them visiting the site more often in order to consume more recommended videos. I would not be surprised if YouTube removes RSS integration in the future, as many feed-based sites such as Facebook and Twitter that used to offer RSS support have eliminated or heavily crippled that feature. You can do a web search to find out if adding a YouTube channel to an RSS feed is still possible and what the latest method is. I don't use YouTube too much — I follow just two YouTube channels via RSS, in addition to occasionally seeking out tutorial videos and product testimonials on the platform — but I understand why "creators" are increasingly moving to video content over written content. That's just where the online audience has migrated as mobile devices have taken over as the primary gateway to the World Wide Web (especially among younger generations). The smartphone media consumer generally wants the ultimate in passive content.

There's no real limit or rule of how many feeds you should follow via RSS. The most obvious variable is how often a particular feed pushes an update; one person could follow a dozen websites that publish an article once or twice per month and have a less-populated RSS feed than someone who follows a single website or YouTube channel that updates daily. It's up to you to monitor and decide how much time that you will spend consuming online content. I'll emphasize again the necessity of seeking a balance between consumption and creation with the various activities in one's life. Personally, my aggregated online content consumption sources are mainly derived from two YouTube channels, four websites, and a dozen podcasts, all of which I have subscribed to via RSS. None update daily; some only a few times per year. I'd estimate that on average I get about one new article, video, or podcast episode appearing in my feed daily (though I do not check or consume online content on a daily basis). Never engage in the sunk cost fallacy with subscriptions — if you've noticed a source going downhill in quality and it doesn't recover after a reasonable period of time, just cut it out of your feed.

Nearly all of the content that you're consuming online while wandering from website to website can be delivered in an RSS feed. This makes the internet's vast ocean of content more like a newspaper that gets delivered to you a few times per week, ready to be picked up and consumed when you have time, and less like the addictive, bottomless feeds served to us by the techno-conglomerates on platforms like Reddit. Contributing free content to these sites instead of starting our own websites and engaging with other independent content creators only perpetuates the current state of the web. Using RSS is a way to recapture the usefulness and educational promise that the internet had around the turn of the twenty-first century, while dodging many of the psychological manipulation tactics and the corporate obsession with ever-increasing "engagement." Eventually we just don't have more time to hand over, and much as I experienced, this may cause people to reach a breaking point where they realize that the amount of time that they were spending online was simply far too large. It would be to all of our benefit to vote with our attention, and intentionally use only those aspects of the World Wide Web which are in agreement with our individual principles and reflect the type of online content that we want to see more of.

Chapter 24
Your New Life

Presupposing that you are successful in quitting or heavily reducing the amount of time you spend scrolling on various websites and apps, if you were an average or above-average user of these platforms, your life going forward will look markedly different. And not only disparate from the most recent years of your own life, but from the current state of many peoples' lives. It was only after becoming aware of my own technology addiction that I began paying attention to similar symptoms in many people that I've interacted with. Things such as having one's phone belching out a near-constant stream of notifications; pulling out said phone at inappropriate moments in a conversation as if it were a behavioral tic to respond to some likely-less-than-urgent text message; withdrawing from interactions to scroll on social media or play some silly phone game; I could continue on but will not belabor the point. When I was a teenager, these were the type of behaviors that baby boomers harped about as being rude, but then most of them got addicted to their phones and computers as well — and the few who didn't probably just got tired of repeating themselves to an audience that was not listening anyway.

Choosing to live your own life more intentionally in this regard is a tacit acceptance of what is currently an uncommon lifestyle in society. Truthfully, it is a less awkward position than may be initially expected, but does require some occasional deftness in social situations. In my experience, most people are somewhat supportive when they attempt to discuss some popular social media platform or the latest hot smartphone app with me and I mention that I'm actually not a user; frequently they let that topic trail off with a regretful comment about how much time they waste on such things. It's important to note that such observations from others are often not an appropriate springboard to launch into a diatribe about all the negative aspects of their platforms of choice and how amazing your life has been since leaving it all behind. I mention this fact solely for the benefit of those who may have a stunted level of social development due to spending far more time on the internet than interacting with actual people, leading to an inability to "read the room" or assess the difference between polite indifference versus conversational interest in a topic.

The zeal of the convert is a term describing the very fervent devotion to new beliefs, which are radically different from one's old beliefs. It is commonly used in regard to religious converts, but is certainly also applicable to those who undertake sweeping changes in their general lifestyle. Many of us have had interactions with people who have dedicated themselves full-bore into new diets, exercise regimens, or twelve-step programs for substance addiction and simply will not stop gushing about it long after their audience has lost any semblance of interest. Forming a core aspect of your identity around the concept of no longer doing something is a slippery slope towards becoming an iconoclast.

Uncompromising absolutism can be a valuable mental tool in specific situations, especially for those who need to break an addiction. But taking the action of quitting web surfing to a Neo-Luddite extreme will be just as irritating and uningratiating as a moderate drinker being forced to listen to the alcoholic relentlessly demonize booze. Share your personal experience and thoughts on this topic earnestly yet humbly when asked, but simply maintain tact in respecting the choices of others, as long as they extend the same courtesy. Most people would likely agree that they spend too much time online, but that's not necessarily an indicator that they're seeking actionable advice to rectify that. Some people may spend five hours or more per day on their smartphone and not even think of it as an issue; that's their prerogative. Others may effortlessly spend a minimal amount of time on the internet daily and feel no addictive pull from it, while another group needs to read an entire book focused on reforming one's digital habits to adopt the same attitude. Everyone ultimately has the autonomy to choose their own path, and in my experience anybody who fails to recognize this never tends to make for interesting conversation.

Critics may occasionally be encountered, which in my opinion is a common manifestation of cognitive dissonance from people who have made some activity a core aspect of their identity but who lack the self-awareness to recognize that it may not be interesting to everybody, or that people simply have different priorities for allocating their time in life. I have been met with consternation from sports fans when they learn that I don't watch sports, from movie and television buffs when I haven't seen some "must-watch" movie or television show and have no clue who such-and-such actor or actress is, or from news junkies when I haven't heard of some national event that is apparently noteworthy despite not tangibly impacting either of our lives. So far I have not been subjected to the same level of reaction when I respond that I unfortunately did not see the latest hilarious meme because I don't go on Reddit or social media platforms, but I would not be surprised if this becomes more commonplace in the future as these platforms suck up ever more of peoples' time and become ingrained in the social fabric to the same degree as the former activities.

Some public arguments are already being presented along the above lines. Lee Rainie and Janna Anderson wrote an article for the *Pew Research Center* in 2017 titled "The Internet of Things Connectivity Binge: What Are the Implications?" wherein one of the major themes brought up by the canvassed respondents was on the difficulty of unplugging.[78] Among the respondents, four people independently brought up the idea that disconnecting would only be for the privileged, with one anonymous Australian professor calling it a "hipster privilege." Another respondent commented that "disconnection and remaining in society are mutually incompatible." Among the responses, I note a general tone of backwardly-justified defeatism. It seems like leaping a logical chasm to conclude that we all might as well succumb to the concept that we will be connected all the time since a few basic tasks like needing an email account to apply for jobs or accessing our bank account require connectivity. Jon Hudson, a principal engineer and self-described futurist, is quoted as saying, "We all must get more and more connected if we want to see where this is going and reach that next level. Whatever it is."[79] I am skeptical that there is a more presumptuous field of thought than futurology; such technology fetishists frequently are either too idealistic or hyperopic to envision potential misuses of technologies, or simply assume that like them, the rest of society should be willing to pay nearly any price for progressively more technological advancement. Only fifteen percent of respondents to this *Pew Research Center* study believed that issues or negative impacts caused by a hyper-connected life would cause people to choose to disconnect.

The argument that one must be privileged in order to disconnect is gradually becoming louder whenever the topic of spending less time online is brought up, but that does not make it more correct. Allison Matyus wrote an article for *Digital Trends* in 2020 with nearly that word-for-word title: "Unplugging From Technology is Now a Privilege."[80] The article, written on the National Day of Unplugging — which is apparently a holiday, and falls on the first Friday of March — argues that one must be privileged to be able to disconnect for just twenty-four hours. While I agree with one of Matyus's points which is that many people rely on technology to perform their job and earn money, the implied conclusion that most people can't find an uninterrupted period of twenty-four hours during which they don't need to work is not borne out by the data.

The US Bureau of Labor Statistics performed a population survey in 2022 which found that among all people who currently work, the average amount of hours worked per week was 38.6. This was remarkably consistent regardless of racial background, with data points for all races surveyed falling within the range of 38.1–38.9 hours per week.[81] The average worker invests time equivalent to just slightly less than a five-day work week at their job and thus has at least the temporal equivalent of two days off per week; whether these days are sequential or fall on the typical weekend days is irrelevant to my counterpoint that *most* people in fact do have the ability to disconnect for twenty-four hours if they so choose, regardless of their racial or socioeconomic background.

Matyus's additional points do not hold up any better to scrutiny, and perhaps the worst reason she presents as to why only the privileged can fully disconnect for a full day is the need for everyone else to use technology "to keep on top of pressing issues in the world." I have previously discussed my own opinions on most news coverage being unactionable rubbish in this book, thus it will come as no surprise to my readers that I disagree with Matyus here. Nobody save perhaps those living in an active war zone will experience any negative effect from disconnecting from most news coverage for the remainder of their lifetime, let alone a single day. And sure, perhaps those of us lucky enough to not live in an area of strife are privileged in the literal definition of the word, but certainly not in the modern day politically-charged sense which is what I interpreted the article's usage to imply. There's also a conflict of interest in reading articles about disconnecting from online life from web-based media outlets who require unfettered access to peoples' attention in order to survive.

Furthermore, this argument that opting out of being connected requires privilege can be written off as a stale farce because it's just a recycled version of the same thing we've heard for much longer (at least in America) in regard to voting. The claim goes that not voting and ignoring politics is a sign of privilege because the consequences of which party wields political power will affect marginalized groups and important issues in society, therefore one who is able to completely ignore this must live in a highly-advantaged, insulated bubble. Again, though, the data disproves this, as Glenn Greenwald revealed in the title of an article for *The Intercept* in 2020: "Nonvoters Are Not Privileged. They Are Disproportionately Lower-Income, Nonwhite, and Dissatisfied With the Two Parties." Citing a *Pew* survey, Greenwald expands, "the most common cause for not registering is that *they do not want to vote*, and the most common reasons have nothing to do with voter suppression and everything to do with beliefs about the worthlessness of the elections. As Pew put it, 'forty-four percent of eligible unregistered individuals say they do not want to vote,' while 'twenty-five percent say they are unregistered because they have not been inspired by a candidate or issue.'"[82]

Freakonomics authors Stephen Dubner and Steven Levitt examined this phenomenon from the perspective of economists in a 2005 *New York Times* article titled "Why Vote?" They write, "Why would an economist be embarrassed to be seen at the voting booth? Because voting exacts a cost – in time, effort, lost productivity – with no discernible payoff except perhaps some vague sense of having done your 'civic duty.' As the economist Patricia Funk wrote in a recent paper, 'A rational individual should abstain from voting.'" They continue by citing data to demonstrate that a single vote is almost never pivotal, most elections aren't even close, and the rare one that is will almost certainly be decided by courts and not the voters.[83]

One thing that Dubner and Levitt neglect to mention is that due to the Electoral College the value of each American's vote in a national election varies wildly depending on which state they live in; if one lives in a "swing state" during an election which is expected to be reasonably close, their vote is worth many magnitudes more than someone who lives in a state in which voters reliably select the same party by a large margin. Since the latter group contains most of the states (and the majority of the United States' population), the majority of the peoples' votes are worth nothing when deciding the outcome. Therefore, a rational American — and economists often consider themselves exemplary at identifying rational choices, if not always implementing them in their personal lives — would simply not waste their time keeping up with political news, educating themselves about the candidates, or ultimately voting if they live in one of the majority of states or districts where their vote for national elections does not truly count. Ironically, people who do get involved in politics typically spend the most time talking about and consuming content related to national politics rather than local elections where their vote ultimately has more weight and the resulting outcome has a larger impact on their day-to-day life.

Those who are defensive of their propensity to waste time on the internet may justify it by saying that "time you enjoyed wasting is not wasted." That statement is true in a general sense, but not in totality. Perhaps scrolling online was not the most enjoyable way in which one could have allocated that period of time. Maybe the greatest total benefit to the individual is not obtained by maximizing enjoyment, but by optimizing their life for multiple metrics including things like self-satisfaction or fulfillment, which cannot be gleaned from the act of passively consuming media. As with many things in life, the correct answer likely comes down to finding a balance that works for the individual. Again, everyone is free to choose their own path, but my primary concern with Reddit and similar time-wasting platforms is that people are becoming addicted to them and having their time stolen by manipulative means, rather than making an intentional, premeditated decision to invest so much time into these sites.

I quit Reddit and other wasteful web surfing because it was good for *me*. I'm not hurting anybody with that decision other than perhaps the techno-conglomerates (and only in the most minuscule way), but they've extracted enough hours of my time to last the rest of my life. When nobody is being tangibly harmed by your course of action, I think it's fair to say that any critics can be safely ignored. Perhaps the real privilege all along was coming from people who sit and write online about how those who don't live exactly according to their standards are privileged. If all of my years on Reddit taught me just one thing, it's that those who are drawn to the massive, unearned audiences of these social media platforms often have the least bit to say worth listening to; people can spew whatever half-baked thoughts or ideas that they have onto their keyboard and find plenty of others with less critical thinking skills than themselves to give them affirmation. Any such people are surely free to take to Reddit, Twitter, or whatever other social media platform to rebuke the whole of what I've written here — I certainly won't be venturing onto those sites to read it.

Ultimately, black and white thinking is the hallmark of an atrophied mind, common among the type of terminally online people who hang out on sites like Reddit. That's not you any longer. You will hopefully eventually gravitate towards others who live similarly, even if moderating technology use is not an explicitly recognized commonality. I'm optimistic that a growing subset of people will continue pushing back against these addictive platforms and choose to disconnect in favor of the real world. You can live differently by taking the middle road — neither a hermit nor a technology addict — a road which these days is lightly traveled. Never compromise on following the path that you know to be the correct one for yourself.

Chapter 25
Relapse and Reflection

In the process of deciding to quit certain platforms that one has used daily for years, relapsing is a likely eventuality for many people. I am certainly not recommending to approach this task with a cynical attitude and an expectation of imminent failure, but any discussion of internet addiction must necessarily address the topic of relapse, save for those few among us who have ironclad willpower. I suspect, however, that many people who claim with bravado that they could quit web browsing, social media, and whatever time-wasting apps they have installed on their phone without a second thought, yet have not actually attempted the task, would find it harder than they expect. Reddit's /r/NoSurf community is littered with a countless (and continuously growing) number of frustrated posts from users who have tried to quit various platforms numerous times and failed when they decided to visit some website of choice again or re-downloaded some app they want to quit using.

Quitting wasteful web browsing is hard, and the task is made more difficult with how few people are acknowledging or discussing internet addiction or, worse, attempting to trivialize it. There is certainly less risk of bodily harm or impact to others compared to substance addictions, and the number of people who have completely ruined their life's course by spending too much time online is probably quite small. But with the average US adult's daily usage time of nearly four hours combined spent consuming media on smartphones, tablets, and computers according to the *Nielsen* report cited in Chapter Nineteen, internet browsing may rank as one of the most widespread socially acceptable addictions in human history. "Smartphone addiction" is really just a subset of internet addiction, because people are using said phones primarily to access internet-based applications and platforms. Ultimately, the discussion should be device-agnostic because those spending too much time on their smartphones exhibit nearly identical behaviors and patterns of use as people like myself who overindulged in online content accessed via a desktop computer.

It doesn't seem like too much of a stretch to speculate that the difficulty of quitting or heavily reducing one's internet use is correlated with the total amount of time that one is spending online. But to be quite frank, even the average amount of time that people are spending on their devices is ludicrous, to the point where I'd conjecture that the majority of people would struggle to quit these habits without relapsing. This second part of the book was the fruit of my experience with repeated failure, reflection, and trying again. I found what works (and what didn't) and I am sharing it so others can hopefully achieve some beneficial acceleration in their journey to reduce their internet use.

Failure is an inherent part of the process in reforming a bad habit or quitting an addiction — whichever level of criticality you feel is personally appropriate to describe overuse of the internet. Many times I would justify to myself that I was going to catch up with hobby-related news on Reddit "for just fifteen minutes" and ended up spending far longer on the site, proceeding to slowly get sucked back into my old habits over the next several days to the point where I was spending two or more hours per day on Reddit again. A few weeks to a couple of months later I would realize that my other goals and projects had been severely negatively impacted by the amount of time that I was spending browsing and I would resolve to quit once more. It honestly took me over two years from the day that I first decided that I *should* quit Reddit and other wasteful web browsing, until I reached the point where I could confidently say that I had accomplished that goal, because not only had I been successful in staying off Reddit for a long period of time but I was also no longer suppressing a desire to go on the site; I simply had no desire to return after enumerating all the negative aspects of the site as well as the positive benefits that I had reaped by quitting.

Failure in the process of aiming to reform our digital habits is neither pointless nor shameful. You presumably succeeded for *some* length of time prior to relapsing, and that time spent away likely ushered in some positive discoveries. Perhaps in your first attempt, you only managed to make it a single day without wasting time online; you may have observed how much longer your evening felt when it wasn't spent scrolling. You probably completed several small tasks that you had been deferring, had time to make and enjoy dinner either alone or with family, then glanced at the clock and realized that it was much earlier in the evening than you expected, leading to an ample amount of time to read a book before heading to bed at a reasonable hour. The next day, you may have woken up more rested than usual due to not engaging in the usual habit of scrolling on your phone before bed.

By the second or third relapse event, you may have made it several days or a couple of weeks without wasting time on the internet. It's conceivable that you've begun to notice positive shifts in your cognitive baseline around that time period, much as I did. You may have noticed your daily mood beginning to uplift after an extended period away from the inundation of negative news and mental pollution wrought by reading the thoughts of irrational, terminally online people. Your ability to concentrate will have likely shown noticeable improvements. Perhaps you've kept yourself busy by establishing a daily habit of engaging in one or more activities or hobbies that you had been putting off because you lied to yourself about "not having the time" and have found it to be a satisfying endeavor.

If you experience failure, those are the positive experiences to think about to force yourself to right your course and get back to what you have to do. To get sucked back into wasting time scrolling on the internet means giving up that more serene, productive, and intentional existence in this world that you had caught a glimpse of during your time away. Once you have mentally acknowledged that a relapse has occurred, continuing down that path is a conscious decision. Doing so is a staunch admission that you were unable to muster enough mental fortitude to quit wasteful browsing — driving the realization that the addictive potential of the internet is likely much higher than one might initially reckon, and that this is a task which most people cannot accomplish passively and instead requires a singular focus to push through those particularly difficult initial days.

Returning to the economic concept of opportunity cost (which states that when one is presented with multiple choices and must pick only one, they are losing the potential gain from the alternative choices relative to the one that was selected), what is not often discussed is that making an optimal decision requires *information*. One needs to know not only all of the choices that can be made, but what the benefits of each choice are. For example, without any knowledge of what someone would spend their time doing if they quit Reddit, the only accurate statement that can be made is that the opportunity cost of using Reddit is that one is not *not* spending their time on Reddit. This is hardly a value-added conclusion, other than for purely demonstrative purposes.

I can provide an account of my experiences and the information that I have learned, which to all others will always be secondhand. But gaining that knowledge yourself will underscore it more strongly than anything relayed from another source. Experiencing relapse necessitates that one has at least started at the task, as compared to not making an attempt at all. Deciding to start is when the true journey commences; any setbacks or failures are a time to reflect on what new information one has gained, to be able to more fully articulate a firsthand opportunity cost of quitting Reddit and other wasteful web browsing. Your takeaways will not necessarily directly mirror mine, though I suspect that the core of my experience will hold true for many people.

Relapse does not mean starting over from zero. Collect yourself and continue on with this task that you initially committed to for several reasons. The best advice that I can provide in this regard is to challenge yourself to make each successive attempt last longer than the previous one. One of the main reasons why I recommended a thirty-day gradual digital detox is because I felt like this uninterrupted period of time away from one's worst technology habit is roughly the amount of time required to notice most of the benefits of quitting or heavily reducing web surfing, as well as to allow positive habits to form around one's chosen replacement activities. There is a minimum amount of time required to break that psychological compulsion to scroll, which in my experience I felt was right around that thirty days, and the first time that I was successful in staying off Reddit for an uninterrupted month was the first time that I truly felt I could declare that I succeeded with this whole endeavor. After I learned what I needed to learn to decide to permanently commit to a more analog lifestyle, then figured out *how* to do so successfully, all of my other time-wasting technology habits quickly fell away.

Once you understand the quality of life that you are missing out on by wasting so much time online through firsthand experience of living beyond the shackles of internet addiction, it's truly difficult to go back. Trading that all in to go back to the mediocre existence of the average person today (and of my former self), wasting evening after evening of their potential just scrolling for hours, is such a lopsided exchange that I refuse to allow it to occur. If you live like that and don't force a reckoning with yourself, you might just scroll your entire life away — and that, I think, is the true opportunity cost of using Reddit and similar platforms.

References and Footnotes

[1]: Patel, Sahil. "Reddit Claims 52 Million Daily Users, Revealing a Key Figure for Social-Media Platforms." *The Wall Street Journal*, Dow Jones & Company, 1 Dec. 2020, https://www.wsj.com/articles/reddit-claims-52-million-daily-users-revealing-a-key-figure-for-social-media-platforms-11606822200.

[2]: "What Is Karma?" *Reddit Help*, https://reddit.zendesk.com/hc/en-us/articles/204511829-What-is-karma.

[3]: Sherman, Lauren E., et al. "The power of the like in adolescence: Effects of peer influence on neural and behavioral responses to social media." *Psychological science* 27.7 (2016): 1027-1035.

[4]: Molapour, Tanaz, et al. "Seven computations of the social brain." *Social Cognitive and Affective Neuroscience* 16.8 (2021): 745-760.

[5]: "Reddiquette." *Reddit Help*, https://reddit.zendesk.com/hc/en-us/articles/205926439-Reddiquette.

[6]: "Reddit.com Traffic Analytics & Market Share." *Similarweb*, https://www.similarweb.com/website/reddit.com/.

[7]: In between the time period when this chapter was written and the publishing of this book, Reddit updated their advertising page to remove this information. The Wayback Machine internet archive project preserves an older version of this page which contains the information as originally cited at https://web.archive.org/web/20220922230439/https://www.redditinc.com/advertising/audience.

[8]: *Udacity*. "Growing Reddit - Web Development." *YouTube*, 27 May 2012, https://www.youtube.com/watch?v=zmeDzx4SUME.

[9]: Hauser, Robert Mason. *Meritocracy, cognitive ability, and the sources of occupational success*. Madison, WI: Center for Demography and Ecology, University of Wisconsin, 2002.

[10]:Ohanian, Alexis. "A Beginner's Guide to Reddit." *Guides.co*, https://guides.co/g/a-beginners-guide-to-reddit/9682.

[11]:Lenssen, Philipp. "A Chat with Aaron Swartz." *Google Blogoscoped*, 7 May 2007, http://blogoscoped.com/archive/2007-05-07-n78.html.

[12]:Suler, John. "The online disinhibition effect." *Cyberpsychology & behavior : the impact of the Internet, multimedia and virtual reality on behavior and society* vol. 7,3 (2004): 321-6.

[13]:Cheng, J., Bernstein, M., Danescu-Niculescu-Mizil, C., & Leskovec, J. (2017). Anyone Can Become a Troll. *Proceedings of the 2017 ACM Conference on Computer Supported Cooperative Work and Social Computing*. https://doi.org/10.1145/2998181.2998213

[14]:Winston, Philip. "GPT-3 Bot Posed as a Human on AskReddit for a Week." *Metastable*, 6 Oct. 2020, https://metastable.org/gpt-3.html.

[15]:Allen, Samantha. "Reddit Is Not the Front Page of the Internet." *The Daily Beast*, 14 Apr. 2017, https://www.thedailybeast.com/reddit-is-not-the-front-page-of-the-internet.

[16]:Bianchi, Tiago. "Regional Distribution of Desktop Traffic to Reddit.com as of May 2022 by Country." *Statista*, 13 Jan. 2023, https://www.statista.com/statistics/325144/reddit-global-active-user-distribution/.

[17]:Ha, Anthony. "Reddit Made $8.3M in Ad Revenue Last Year, and It Will Donate 10 Percent to Charity." *TechCrunch*, 18 Feb. 2015, https://techcrunch.com/2015/02/18/reddit-charity/.

[18]:Bobrowsky, Meghan. "Reddit Valuation Soars to $10 Billion in New Funding Round." *The Wall Street Journal*, Dow Jones & Company, 12 Aug. 2021, https://www.wsj.com/articles/reddit-taps-investor-appetite-for-startups-further-raising-valuation-11628766000.

[19]:"Facebook Reports Fourth Quarter and Full Year 2020 Results." *Meta Investor Relations*, https://investor.fb.com/investor-news/press-release-details/2021/Facebook-Reports-Fourth-Quarter-and-Full-Year-2020-Results/default.aspx.

[20]:*Meta Investor Relations - Press Releases*, https://investor.fb.com/investor-news/default.aspx.

[21]:*Twitter, Inc. - Financial Information - Quarterly Results*, https://investor.twitterinc.com/financial-information/quarterly-results/.

[22]:*Snap Inc. - Financials - Quarterly Results*, https://investor.snap.com/financials/quarterly-results/default.aspx.

[23]:"Is There an #Adlergic Epidemic? Ad Blocking across Media." *Deloitte Global*, https://www2.deloitte.com/content/dam/Deloitte/global/Images/infographics/technologymediatelecommunications/gx-deloitte-tmt-2018-adblocking-media-report.pdf.

[24]:"Series F - Reddit - 2021-08-12." *Crunchbase*, https://www.crunchbase.com/funding_round/reddit-series-f–1adb717d.

[25]:Cheema, Sonia, and Noor Zainab Hussain. "Reddit Jumps on IPO Bandwagon with Confidential Filing." *Reuters*, Thomson Reuters, 16 Dec. 2021, https://www.reuters.com/markets/us/reddit-files-us-ipo-2021-12-16/.

[26]:Roof, Katie, and Crystal Tse. "Reddit Picks Banks for IPO (MS, GS)." *Bloomberg*, 7 Jan. 2022, https://www.bloomberg.com/news/articles/2022-01-07/reddit-is-said-to-tap-morgan-stanley-goldman-sachs-for-ipo.

[27]:Weinberg, Cory. "Reddit Aims for IPO in Second Half as Market's Gears Quietly Turn." *The Information*, 15 Feb. 2023, https://www.theinformation.com/articles/reddit-aims-for-ipo-in-second-half-as-markets-gears-quietly-turn.

[28]:Stokes, Samantha. "Stripe, Reddit and Instacart Valuations Take a Beating in Fidelity's Latest Markdowns. Here's How They Fared." *Business Insider*, https://www.businessinsider.com/fidelity-marks-down-stripe-reddit-and-instacart-valuations-2023-1.

[29]:Kreider, Tim. "Isn't It Outrageous?" *The New York Times*, 14 July 2009, https://archive.nytimes.com/opinionator.blogs.nytimes.com/2009/07/14/isnt-it-outrageous/.

[30]:An aside: the posts that receive the most karma points in /r/UnpopularOpinion tend to actually be quite popular opinions (at least among Reddit's demographic), and several Redditors have pointed out this hypocrisy in the past. We discussed in Chapter Two how Redditors use the karma voting system to upvote posts that they already agree with and downvote those that they disagree with. The purpose of /r/UnpopularOpinion was

originally to inverse this behavior, however with millions of subscribers this community long ago lost the plot. As a result, *actual* unpopular opinions posted to that community tend to get little to no traction.

[31]:Brady WJ, Wills JA, Jost JT, Tucker JA, Van Bavel JJ. Emotion shapes the diffusion of moralized content in social networks. *Proc Natl Acad Sci USA*. 2017 Jul 11; 114(28):7313-7318.

[32]:Berger J, Milkman KL. What Makes Online Content Viral? *Journal of Marketing Research*. 2012;49(2):192-205.

[33]:M. J. Crockett, Moral outrage in the digital age. *Nat. Hum. Behav.* **1**, 769–771 (2017).

[34]:Hofmann, W., Wisneski, D. C., Brandt, M. J. & Skitka, L. J. Morality in everyday life. *Science*. (New York, NY) **345**, 1340–1343 (2014).

[35]:McCarthy, Caroline. "Conde Nast's Reddit Goes Open-Source." *CNET*, 18 June 2008, https://www.cnet.com/culture/conde-nasts-reddit-goes-open-source/.

[36]:"What's a Moderator?" *Reddit Help*, https://reddit.zendesk.com/hc/en-us/articles/204533859-What-s-a-moderator.

[37]:Pathak, Shareen. "Reddit Hates Marketing. How to Market on It Anyway." *Ad Age*, 10 Mar. 2014, https://adage.com/article/special-report-sxsw/reddit-hates-marketing-market/292068.

[38]:Pitman, Jamie. "Local Consumer Review Survey 2022: Customer Reviews and Behavior." *BrightLocal*, 23 Jan. 2023, https://www.brightlocal.com/research/local-consumer-review-survey/.

[39]:Bazilian, Emma. "Infographic: How Millennials and Baby Boomers Consume User-Generated Content." *Adweek*, 2 Jan. 2017, https://www.adweek.com/brand-marketing/infographic-how-millennials-and-baby-boomers-consume-user-generated-content-175307/.

[40]:The context of this statement is that it was directed at moderators of the /r/science community, who were temporarily removing user-submitted posts to boost the visibility of Ask Me Anything (AMA) question-and-answer threads with various guests. When they saw traffic on these posts drop drastically, the moderators of /r/science claimed that Reddit was "taking actions behind the scenes to kill the visibility of our AMAs." What actually happened was that Reddit had recently discontinued the practice of curating a list of default subreddits (of which /r/science was one) which had for years given this list of communities higher visibility at the expense of other subreddits. Instead, the /r/popular feed was introduced to put subreddits on a more even playing field, which is when /r/science saw their traffic drop off. Essentially the moderators of this community (primarily users "nallen" and "nate") did not understand or did not want to believe that their content was less interesting to users when they were not forced to see it by virtue of /r/science being a default subreddit, and engaged in this method of vote manipulation to attempt to maintain the relative standing among other communities that they had unfairly enjoyed previously.

[41]:Savchuk, Katia. "Are America's Richest Families Republicans or Democrats?" *Forbes*, Forbes Magazine, 12 Oct. 2022, https://www.forbes.com/sites/katiasavchuk/2014/07/09/are-americas-richest-families-republicans-or-democrats/?sh=6d398c053e83.

[42]:"Advance Publications Profile: Contributions Totals." *OpenSecrets*, https://www.opensecrets.org/orgs/advance-publications/totals?id=D000041920.

[43]:Ohlheiser, Abby, and Hayley Tsukayama. "Reddit's CEO Regrets Trolling Trump Supporters by Secretly Editing Their Posts." *The Washington Post*, 5 Dec. 2021, https://www.washingtonpost.com/news/the-switch/wp/2016/11/26/reddits-ceo-regrets-trolling-trump-supporters-by-secretly-editing-their-posts/.

[44]:Kravets, David. "Reddit CEO Who Altered Comments Apologizes, Unveils Subreddit Filtering." *Ars Technica*, 30 Nov. 2016, https://arstechnica.com/tech-policy/2016/11/reddit-ceo-issues-mea-culpa-unveils-proactive-approach-to-site-policing/?comments=1&comments-page=1.

[45]:*Point*. "Reddit for Sale: How We Bought the Top Spot for $200 (Reupload)." *YouTube*, 26 Sept. 2018, https://www.youtube.com/watch?v=6SAkUs3urrg.

[46]:Tait, Amelia. "Some of Reddit's Wildest Relationship Stories Are Lies. I'd Know – I Wrote Them." *Vice*, 13 July 2020, https://www.vice.com/en/article/4ay4vn/reddit-relationships-fake-stories-authors.

[47]:Roser, Max, and Esteban Ortiz-Ospina. "Literacy." *Our World in Data*, University of Oxford, 13 Aug. 2016, https://ourworldindata.org/literacy.

[48]:Ritchie, Hannah, and Max Roser. "Technology Adoption." *Our World in Data*, University of Oxford, 2 Oct. 2017, https://ourworldindata.org/technology-adoption.

[49]:Boot, A.B., Tjong Kim Sang, E., Dijkstra, K. *et al.* How character limit affects language usage in tweets. *Palgrave Communications* **5,** 76 (2019).

[50]:"Fact Sheet: An Adjustment to Global Poverty Lines." *World Bank*, 16 Sept. 2022, https://www.worldbank.org/en/news/factsheet/2022/05/02/fact-sheet-an-adjustment-to-global-poverty-lines.

[51]:Alós-Ferrer, Carlos, et al. "Inertia and Decision Making." *Frontiers in Psychology*, vol. 7, 2016, https://doi.org/10.3389/fpsyg.2016.00169.

[52]:This quote is sourced from Elizabeth Carter's translation of *The Enchiridion*, which is in the public domain.

[53]:Johnson, Samuel. "No. 2. The necessity and danger of looking into futurity." *The Rambler*, March 24, 1750.

[54]:Hofmann, W., Baumeister, R. F., Förster, G., & Vohs, K. D. (2012). Everyday temptations: An experience sampling study of desire, conflict, and self-control. *Journal of Personality and Social Psychology, 102*(6), 1318–1335.

[55]:Dixon, S. "Daily Time Spent on Social Networking by Internet Users Worldwide from 2012 to 2022." *Statista*, 22 Aug. 2022, https://www.statista.com/statistics/433871/daily-social-media-usage-worldwide/.

[56]: Unless, that is, they stood to benefit in some other way, such as financially. I have gone back and forth on whether it would be hypocritical of me to return to Reddit and make a single post in /r/NoSurf announcing (advertising) the completion of my book. Clearly my motivations would not be completely altruistic (else I would offer the book for free), but I would also like for this offline resource to have a chance to get into the hands of those who may need it most rather than simply be ignored, as first releases from self-published authors so frequently are. I have concluded that a single post fully disclosing my own interest (and adhering to US FTC guidelines) is a fair compensation for the years of inauthentic, illegal astroturfing that I experienced as a user of Reddit.

[57]: Watson, Meg. "Why Your Friends Are Disappearing from Your Instagram Feed." *The Sydney Morning Herald*, 24 July 2022, https://www.smh.com.au/technology/why-your-friends-are-disappearing-from-your-instagram-feed-20220719-p5b2wu.html.

[58]: SensorTower, 2020, *Q4 2019 Store Intelligence Data Digest*, https://go.sensortower.com/rs/351-RWH-315/images/Sensor-Tower-Q4-2019-Data-Digest.pdf.

[59]: "Tiktok Named as the Most Downloaded App of 2020." *BBC News*, BBC, 10 Aug. 2021, https://www.bbc.com/news/business-58155103.

[60]: Koetsier, John. "10 Most Downloaded Apps of 2022: Facebook down, Spotify up, Tiktok Stable, Capcut Keeps Growing." *Forbes*, Forbes Magazine, 5 Jan. 2023, https://www.forbes.com/sites/johnkoetsier/2023/01/04/top-10-most-downloaded-apps-of-2022-facebook-down-spotify-up-tiktok-stable-capcut-keeps-growing/.

[61]: Shearer, Elisa, and Amy Mitchell. "News Use across Social Media Platforms in 2020." *Pew Research Center*, 9 Feb. 2022, https://www.pewresearch.org/journalism/2021/01/12/news-use-across-social-media-platforms-in-2020/.

[62]: Newman, Nic. "Overview and Key Findings of the 2022 Digital News Report." *Reuters Institute for the Study of Journalism*, 15 June 2022, https://reutersinstitute.politics.ox.ac.uk/digital-news-report/2022/dnr-executive-summary.

[63]: Brenan, Megan. "Americans' Trust in Media Remains near Record Low." *Gallup*, 17 Nov. 2022, https://news.gallup.com/poll/403166/americans-trust-media-remains-near-record-low.aspx.

[64]: Musetti, Alessandro, and Paola Corsano. "The Internet Is Not a Tool: Reappraising the Model for Internet-Addiction Disorder Based on the Constraints and Opportunities of the Digital Environment." *Frontiers in Psychology*, 18 Apr. 2018, https://www.frontiersin.org/articles/10.3389/fpsyg.2018.00558/full.

[65]: The Nielsen Company, 2021, *The Nielsen Total Audience Report*, https://www.nielsen.com/insights/2021/total-audience-advertising-across-todays-media/.

[66]: OECD (2023), Employment rate by age group (indicator). doi: 10.1787/084f32c7-en.

[67]:This quote is sourced from Richard M. Gummere's translation of Seneca's Moral Letters to Lucilius (Latin: *Seneca ad Lucilium Epistulae Morales*), which is in the public domain.

[68]:Haidt, J., & Twenge, J. (ongoing). Social media and mental health: A collaborative review. Unpublished manuscript, New York University. Accessed at tinyurl.com/SocialMediaMentalHealthReview.

[69]:Papworth, S., Rist, J., Coad, L. and Milner-Gulland, E. (2009), Evidence for shifting baseline syndrome in conservation. Conservation Letters, 2: 93-100.

[70]:Blades, Robin. "Protecting the brain against bad news." *CMAJ : Canadian Medical Association journal = journal de l'Association medicale canadienne* vol. 193,12 (2021): E428-E429. doi:10.1503/cmaj.1095928.

[71]:Sacerdote, Bruce, et al. "Why Is All COVID-19 News Bad News?" *Dartmouth College*, 2021. Working paper. Accessed at: https://bpb-us-e1.wpmucdn.com/sites.dartmouth.edu/dist/4/2318/files/2021/03/Why-Is-All-Covid-News-Bad-News-3_22_21.pdf.

[72]:Brereton, Dmitri. "Google Search Is Dying." *DKB*, 15 Feb. 2022, https://dkb.io/post/google-search-is-dying.

[73]:According to web hosting service Zyro, based on data gathered and analyzed from *SimilarWeb* in May 2021. Accessed at https://zyro.com/websites-time.

[74]:Khalid, Asma. "The Father of the Web Is Worried about How Ugly It's Become." *NPR*, 4 Apr. 2017, https://www.npr.org/sections/alltechconsidered/2017/04/04/522593360/the-father-of-the-web-is-worried-about-how-ugly-its-become.

[75]:Horowitz-Ghazi, Alexi, and Sarah Gonzalez, hosts. "How the Cookie Became a Monster." *Planet Money*, NPR, 2022, https://www.npr.org/2022/11/18/1137657496/third-party-cookie-data-tracking-internet-user-privacy.

[76]:"US: Podcast Listeners 2017-2024." *Statista*, 23 Feb. 2022, https://www.statista.com/forecasts/1123105/statista-amo-podcast-reach-us.

[77]:Barrett, Brian. "It's Time for an RSS Revival." *Wired*, Conde Nast, 30 Mar. 2018, https://www.wired.com/story/rss-readers-feedly-inoreader-old-reader/.

[78]:Rainie, Lee, and Janna Anderson. "The Internet of Things Connectivity Binge: What Are the Implications?" *Pew Research Center*, 15 Sept. 2022, https://www.pewresearch.org/internet/2017/06/06/the-internet-of-things-connectivity-binge-what-are-the-implications/.

[79]:Rainie, Lee, and Janna Anderson. "Theme 2: Unplugging Isn't Easy Now, and by 2026 It Will Be Even Tougher." *Pew Research Center*, 15 Sept. 2022, https://www.pewresearch.org/internet/2017/06/06/theme-2-unplugging-isnt-easy-now-and-by-2026-it-will-be-even-tougher/.

[80]:Matyus, Allison. "Unplugging from Technology Is Now a Privilege." *Digital Trends*, 6 Mar. 2020, https://www.digitaltrends.com/news/national-day-of-unplugging-luxury-privilege/.

[81]:"Table 22: Persons at Work in Nonagricultural Industries by Age, Sex, Race, Hispanic or Latino Ethnicity, Marital Status, and Usual Full- or Part-Time Status." *Labor Force Statistics from the Current Population Survey*, U.S. Bureau of Labor Statistics, 25 Jan. 2023, https://www.bls.gov/cps/cpsaat22.htm.

[82]:Greenwald, Glenn. "Nonvoters Are Not Privileged. They Are Disproportionately Lower-Income, Nonwhite, and Dissatisfied With the Two Parties." The Intercept, 9 Apr. 2020, https://theintercept.com/2020/04/09/nonvoters-are-not-privileged-they-are-largely-lower-income-non-white-and-dissatisfied-with-the-two-parties/.

[83]:Dubner, Stephen J., and Steven D. Levitt. "Why Vote?" The New York Times, 6 Nov. 2005, https://www.nytimes.com/2005/11/06/magazine/why-vote.html.

About the Author

Jacob Desforges is an engineer and now also an author. *You Should Quit Reddit* is his first book. A lifelong New Englander, Jacob lives in Massachusetts with his lovely fiancée. You can keep up with his latest projects or get in contact on his website at www.jacobdesforges.com.